DOWN SOUTH

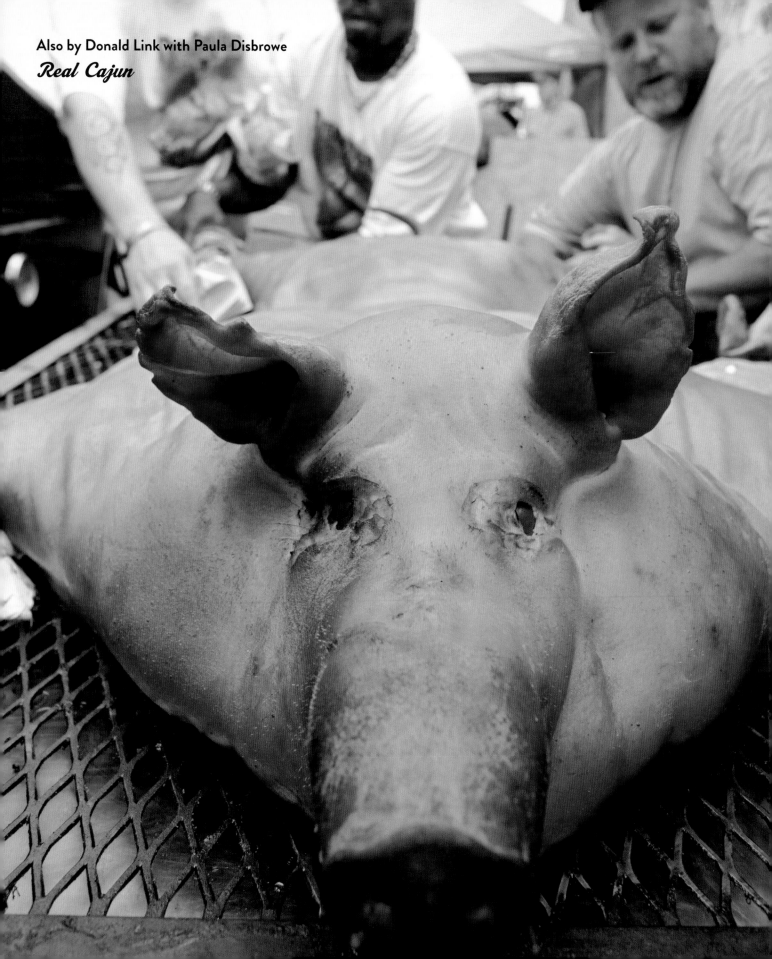

Donald Link

DOWN SOUTH

BOURBON, PORK, GULF SHRIMP & SECOND HELPINGS *of* EVERYTHING

with PAULA DISBROWE | photographs by Chris Granger

Clarkson Potter

NEW YORK

Published in the United States by Clarkson Potter/
Publishers, an imprint of the Crown Publishing Group,
a division of Random House LLC, a Penguin Random
House Company, New York.
www.crownpublishing.com
www.clarksonpotter.com

Library of Congress Cataloging-in-Publication Data
Link, Donald.
   Down south : bourbon, pork, gulf shrimp, and second
helpings of everything / Donald Link
with Paula Disbrowe.
   pages cm

1. Cooking, American—Southern style. 2. Cooking,
Cajun. I. Disbrowe, Paula. II. Title.
TX827.L64 2013
   641.5975—dc23

                                    2013020280

ISBN 978-0-7704-3318-5
eBook ISBN 978-0-7704-3319-2

Printed in Hong Kong

Book design by Jan Derevjanik and Stephanie Huntwork
Cover design by Stephanie Huntwork
Cover photographs by Chris Granger

10 9 8 7 6 5 4 3 2 1

First Edition

I dedicate this book
TO EVERYONE WITH WHOM I HAVE
RAISED A GLASS, COOKED OUT, FISHED,
HUNTED, AND STAYED UP TOO LATE.
I DEDICATE THIS BOOK TO THE SOUTH.

Contents

INTRODUCTION 9

Let's Start with
a Drink 12

OLD-SCHOOL
SOUTHERN
COCKTAIL PARTIES 32

Cook It Outside 62

ROAST, BRAISE,
SIMMER, AND FRY 90

Heads, Feet, Necks,
and Bones 110

SEAFOOD FROM
THE GULF AND
SOUTH ATLANTIC 140

Fresh, Seasonal
Southern Sides 182

SOUTHERN-STYLE
SWEETS 206

ACKNOWLEDGMENTS 250

INDEX 251

Introduction

"I'm going back down South now." It's a line from my favorite band, the Kings of Leon. For me the lyrics, especially cued to a guitar, stir up strong feelings, a yearning for a very specific place and our way of life here. My life in the South—the birthplace of Elvis, the blues, jazz, rock and roll, and country music—is cued to a soundtrack that includes everything from "Freebird," the anthem at our high school parties (where we'd meet up in the country and drink beer), to the song "Whipping Post," the background music for shooting pool and wearing my favorite cowboy boots at the Gator Bar (a classic backwoods dive) in Baton Rouge. There aren't words to describe what it's like staring out at the stars from the back of a pickup, on a warm summer night, while "Seven Bridges Road" by the Eagles plays on the radio.

This cookbook is a collection of remembrances and recipes meant to make you hungry, make you laugh, and convey what it's like to be both a chef and an eater in today's South. This region is part of my DNA in a way that you can't explain to someone who wasn't raised here, but every Southerner knows exactly what I'm talking about. It's about growing up shooting rifles, hunting, fishing, engaging in heated BB gun wars, launching fireworks at each other, drinking beer with the boys, water-skiing in snake-infested rivers, eating fried chicken and cornbread, and admiring beautiful girls in cowboy hats and boots. It's a place where people can cut up and be themselves. It's rowdy, good-natured fun seasoned by deep flavors and a distinct culture.

Not everyone's story is the same, but there's a common thread that connects people who grew up here. The South lives in me just as much as it does in this guy named Skoots whom I met on Florida's northwest coast. He used to work as soundman for the Allman Brothers (giving him major Southern street cred) and as a guitar tech for Deep Purple (he still carries a silver cigarette lighter that lead guitarist Steve Morse gave him). We met incidentally, because we'd rented beach houses next door to each other, but it didn't take long for us to be sharing cans of Bud, stories of fishing, guitar legends, and grilled scallops in the driveway. Southern hospitality is not a myth—it's real.

Along with the soundtrack of life in the South, there's a menu, steeped in fresh Gulf seafood, cured meats, and deeply flavored family meals. It's impossible for me to say which part of the South has the *best* food, because each place has its own soul. Smoked Texas lamb is hard to beat when you're out on a ranch by a crackling campfire, and the two ranch hands you just met pull out guitars and a bottle of bourbon. Then again, so is slow-smoked Memphis barbecue, when you're surrounded by hundreds of smoking pits at Memphis in May, and hanging out with good friends alongside the mud-brown Mississippi River. And there is the great swath of South Louisiana with its gumbo, spicy boiled crawfish, sausage, and boudin. We all know I'm a little biased on this one. Keep driving east and you'll arrive on the Gulf coasts of Mississippi, Alabama, and Florida, all bountiful with baskets of buttery peel-and-eat shrimp, gorgeous beaches, and excellent fishing. Somehow my life in the South has focused mostly on the coastal regions, and that's where you'll find most of my influences come from.

Southern food has changed from when I was younger. The meals that we ate at home while I was growing up—prepared almost exclusively from local ingredients and my grandfather's garden—are not what you'll find on most dinner tables these days. Because of the fast, frenetic lives we all lead, people just don't cook from scratch as much as they used to. If you do stumble on a true home-cooked meal, it's a treat in a big way.

An encouraging thing that I have seen in the last few years is a movement back to the small-scale, local farming that seemed lost for some time to industrialized agriculture. It's definitely a national movement, but those trends don't always reach here. But with a passionate devotion to seasonal, locally driven fare, Southern chefs have changed the landscape of what food is in the South, and have shown the national media that it's not all fried chicken and cornbread. We enjoy a bounty of unique, satisfying ingredients (e.g., farm-raised pork, shell beans, butter beans, peanuts, peaches, okra, tomatoes, hot peppers, and an absurd amount of seafood) that lend themselves to infinite variation, and meals that run the gamut from Black Pepper Biscuits with Country Ham (page 56) to Salted Caramel Peanut Brittle Ice Cream (page 214).

As a chef and owner of several restaurants, I am constantly working to bring out the best of these ingredients in fresh ways that still maintain the soul of Southern cooking and the rich, deep flavors that I grew up with. I've spent my life and career on the road, a journey that's taken me from the oyster shell driveways of Louisiana to the most refined restaurants in the world. The travel has informed my cooking and helped me understand who I am, as both a Southerner and a cook. I've eaten some amazing food and seen some incredible places, but eventually I long to get *back down South*. I yearn for my people and my home, and especially for its food. It's me. *It's a Southern thing.*

Let's Start with a
DRINK

Meyer Lemon French 75 16

HERBSAINT CHAMPAGNE
COCKTAIL 18

Chuck Berry 19

LOUISIANA HAYRIDE 20

Free Cochon Payton 21

FLORA-BAMA RUM
PUNCH 22

A Clockwork Orange 24

KING STREET DERBY 25

St. Edwards No. 1 26

COPPERHEAD 27

Julia Reed's Scotch
Old-Fashioned 29

ANTIGUAN JULEP 30

Deer Stand Old-Fashioned 31

Salty, sand-dusted beach shacks along the Gulf Coast. Sweaty backyard barbecues and crawfish boils with the Black Keys blaring. Freeze-your-ass-off deer hunts and balmy evening fishing trips.

In my hometown of New Orleans, there's an elixir of options that range from fancy cocktail parties in the Garden District to a random sunny afternoon on St. Charles Avenue. It's hard to imagine kicking back with friends anywhere—anytime—in the South without cranking music and imbibing some sort of adult beverage. Lucky for us booze, like food, is relished with gusto.

In the last couple of years, the craft cocktail trend has exploded in cities across the South. While I'm not one for affectation, the bars that do it right, with an understanding of historic context and a reliance on quality small-batch ingredients, serve some pretty spectacular drinks. It's worth the fuss at home, too—a balanced, well-made cocktail that relies on fresh citrus juice, infused simple syrups, aromatic bitters, and quality spirits is a world apart from a sloppy drink.

This chapter shakes up a mix of my favorite libations, many of them tied to great memories, from the lethal rum punch at the Flora-bama (see page 22) to my friend Julia Reed's Scotch Old-Fashioned (see page 29).

Whether you want an elegant aperitif to spark appetites and kick off a dinner party (look no further than the Meyer Lemon French 75), or a potent cocktail to warm your body and fuel conversation (try the Copperhead, I dare you), these recipes will ensure, like any good Southern gentleman, that you won't go thirsty.

All of the recipes in this chapter make one drink, so you measure carefully and get just the right balance of flavors.

A NOTE ON BOURBON

As much as I love cocktails made with whiskey, I have to say that I'm more of a purist with single-barrel bourbon—especially when it comes to Pappy Van Winkle. On a number of occasions, I've had the honor and privilege to drink it from the bottle that his grandson and successor, Julian Van Winkle, carries in his back pocket. Julian is loved and revered throughout the food industry, but he also pisses a lot of people off because he just doesn't have the supply for everyone.

For me, the best way to drink Pappy is with one or two ice cubes. You want to chill the bourbon without watering it down. If you want to really piss off Julian, pour some Coke in your bourbon. You might as well take a dump on the floor, although that might be less of an offense.

THIS CLASSIC COCKTAIL is made from gin, Champagne, lemon juice, and sugar (although the spirit is disputed: Some recipes call for it to be made with brandy or Cognac, which would make it even more French). The recipe can be traced to a bar in Paris, circa 1915. The potent combination of ingredients was said to have such a kick that it compared to being shelled with the powerful French 75mm field gun. Harry Craddock, author of *The Savoy Cocktail Book,* wrote that it "hits with remarkable precision." It's true that this easy-to-drink, deceptively light aperitif sneaks up on you.

I prefer using Meyer lemons because they are less acidic and have a subtly sweeter orange perfume, making them ideal for an aromatic cocktail.

MEYER LEMON
French 75

1 ounce freshly squeezed Meyer lemon juice

½ ounce Basic Simple Syrup (recipe follows)

1½ ounces gin, preferably a London dry style

Champagne or sparkling wine

Twist of Meyer lemon peel

Combine the Meyer lemon juice, simple syrup, and gin in a cocktail shaker with a scoop of ice. Cover and shake vigorously. Pour the strained drink into a flute or coupe glass. Top with Champagne and garnish with the lemon peel.

Basic Simple Syrup

MAKES ABOUT ¾ CUP (6 OUNCES)

½ cup sugar

Heat the sugar and ½ cup water in a small saucepan over medium-high heat, stirring until the sugar has dissolved. Bring the mixture to a boil, then remove from the heat and let cool. Simple syrup can be stored in the refrigerator in a sealed container for several months.

HERBSAINT, THE NAMESAKE spirit of my first restaurant, is an anise-flavored liqueur originally made in New Orleans in the 1930s. The recipe is credited to J. Marion Legendre and Reginald Parker, who learned how to make absinthe when they served France during World War I. Herbsaint, an absinthe substitute, was first sold after the repeal of Prohibition. I like it paired with Champagne and a whiff of berry flavor in this elegant aperitif (our riff on a Kir royale). Crème de mûre is a liqueur flavored with blackberries, though you could also use crème de cassis, made from black currants. While a dry cava or sparkling blanc de noir is an acceptable substitution, for the very best flavor you should splurge on real Champagne.

HERBSAINT
Champagne Cocktail

½ ounce crème de mûre
Splash of Herbsaint
Champagne
Twist of lemon peel

Combine the crème de mûre and Herbsaint in a champagne flute and then fill the remainder of the glass with Champagne. Rub the rim of the flute with the lemon twist and drop it into the cocktail.

I LOVE THE cocktails that come out of Cochon Butcher, the casual sandwich- and charcuterie-driven shop around the corner from my restaurant Cochon. The managers have free rein over the creation and naming of these concoctions, and I'm not sure which I enjoy more—the drinks or the names they come up with. This particular combination is one of my all-time favorites, especially on a hot summer day when the bright, clean flavors are so refreshing, and maybe a little too easy to put down. Which makes it perfect.

CHUCK
Berry

1 tablespoon Blueberry Syrup (recipe follows)

6 fresh blueberries

3 basil leaves

2 lime slices

1 ounce St. Germain elderflower liqueur

Prosecco (or other sparkling wine)

In a rocks glass, muddle the blueberry syrup, blueberries, basil leaves, and lime slices. Fill the glass with ice, then add the St. Germain, and top with sparkling wine; stir to combine.

Blueberry Syrup

MAKES ABOUT 1¾ CUPS (14 OUNCES)

For the best flavor, the blueberry syrup should be made a day in advance. Refrigerate leftovers (the syrup will keep for a couple weeks) and use in other cocktails, in fresh lemonade, or drizzled over vanilla ice cream.

1 pint blueberries

1 cup white vinegar

1 cup sugar

In a nonreactive saucepan, combine the blueberries and vinegar and allow the mixture to macerate at room temperature for 24 hours. The next day, heat the mixture just to the point of boiling. Let cool, then strain the liquid from the pulp, and discard the pulp. Combine the blueberry liquid and sugar in a small saucepan and simmer until reduced and syrupy (the mixture should have the consistency of warm honey), about 20 minutes. Let cool.

LOUISIANA HAYRIDE **WAS** a live radio show in Louisiana in the 1930s that featured countless country music legends, including Hank Williams. Bourbon, warming apple liqueur, and cinnamon-scented simple syrup give this drink comforting fall flavors.

LOUISIANA
Hayride

1 ounce bourbon, preferably Rebel Yell

1 ounce apple liqueur, preferably Laird's applejack brandy

1 ounce peach liqueur, preferably Mathilde Pêches liqueur

1 ounce Cinnamon Simple Syrup (recipe follows)

Splash of fresh lemon juice

Ground cinnamon, for garnish

Fill a cocktail shaker with ice (preferably crushed) and add the bourbon, apple liqueur, peach liqueur, simple syrup, and lemon juice. Shake vigorously and serve over additional ice in an old-fashioned glass. Garnish with a dash of cinnamon.

Cinnamon Simple Syrup

MAKES ABOUT 1¼ CUPS (10 OUNCES)

1 cup sugar
3 cinnamon sticks

Combine the sugar, cinnamon sticks, and 1 cup water in a small saucepan. Bring the mixture to a simmer over medium heat, stirring occasionally, and cook until the sugar is fully dissolved. Set aside for 1 hour to allow the cinnamon flavor to further develop, then strain, and discard the cinnamon sticks. Store leftover syrup in a covered container in the refrigerator for up to 1 month.

AS ANY SELF-RESPECTING Saints fan knows, the name of this cocktail is a play on the local mantra Free Sean Payton, which references the horribly unfair treatment of our much-loved football coach by the NFL. In response to the Bounty scandal (he was accused of offering extra cash payouts to his team in exchange for roughing up key opposing players), Payton was banned from coaching the Saints for an entire season, and unfortunately (but not surprisingly) we then had little hope of making it to the playoffs. The cocktail can be used to ease any pains that season may have caused for fellow Saints fans.

FREE
Cochon Payton

1½ ounces bourbon, preferably Buffalo Trace

2 dashes of Angostura bitters

1 ounce prepared limeade

Splash of Cherry Bounce (recipe follows), plus 1 marinated cherry

Lime wedge

Fill a rocks glass with ice, add the bourbon, bitters, limeade, and cherry bounce, and stir to combine. Garnish with the lime and marinated cherry.

Cherry Bounce

MAKES 1 CUP (8 OUNCES)

Cherry bounce is an eighteenth-century English liqueur made by infusing brandy or another spirit (some people use rum or vodka; I prefer bourbon) with cherries and sugar. When the Crescent City Farmer's Market is brimming with cherries, we preserve them with this simple recipe, which results in a delicious cocktail ingredient (or ice cream topper) all year long.

8 ounces cherries, pitted

1 tablespoon sugar

About 6 ounces bourbon, preferably Buffalo Trace

Fill an 8-ounce Mason jar with pitted cherries. Add the sugar and gently stir. Fill the jar with bourbon to cover the cherries. Shake well and store for up to 6 months at room temperature.

CERTAIN COCKTAILS HAVE an immediate sense of place. Martinis should be sipped in old hotel bars, French rosé at alfresco lunches, and rum punch on the beach. There's no better place to drink the latter than the Flora-bama, a rough and rowdy, multitiered labyrinth of live music, picnic tables, and booze that straddles the border of Florida and Alabama. It's my kind of place—you can dig your toes into the sand, or perch yourself on a patio and shotgun a beer with a view of the Gulf. You can even go to church there on Sunday (I'm not making that up).

When I'm at a beach bar, I immediately slip into vacation mode, and I shamelessly love the let's-get-a-buzz-going-quick fix of a fruity rum punch. This is the Flora-bama's version (complete with their rum preferences)—feel free to change up the rum to suit your taste. Use freshly squeezed citrus juice for the best flavor.

FLORA-BAMA
Rum Punch

½ ounce Bacardi light rum

½ ounce Captain Morgan Original Spiced Rum

¼ ounce Malibu rum

Splash of orange juice

Splash of pineapple juice

Splash of grenadine

Maraschino cherry

Orange slice

Combine all rums, the juices, and grenadine in a tall glass (or plastic cup). Add ice, stir to combine, and garnish with the maraschino cherry and orange slice.

I KNOW I'M biased, but I think New Orleans has the best bars in the country. Neal Bodenheimer, the owner of Cure and Bellocq (a sultry bar devoted to cocktails from the late 1800s), has created some of the smartest and most appealing drinks around. The cocktails at both bars are expertly crafted, and showcase neglected spirits like vermouth, along with obscure ingredients like Benedictine and Chartreuse.

A CLOCKWORK
Orange

1 ounce Regan's Orange Bitters No. 6

1 ounce Grand Marnier

½ ounce Cognac, preferably Pierre Ferrand

2 thick strips of orange peel

5 red or green grapes

Combine the bitters, Grand Marnier, Cognac, and 1 orange peel in a cocktail shaker. Add a scoop of ice and shake 20 times, until well blended. Strain the drink over crushed ice into a cup (a metal or silver cup if you like to roll that way), express the second peel over the drink, and garnish with the peel (see Note). Put the 5 grapes on top of the ice and add appropriately sized straws to the drink.

NOTES: When you don't have a fancy fridge with an ice crusher, I recommend a lint-free kitchen towel and an everyday kitchen item that can be repurposed as a club (such as a meat mallet). Wrap the ice tightly in the towel, put on a sturdy surface, and relieve stress via transference.

To express citrus peel, gently twist the peel into a corkscrew shape; your goal is to spray the oil from the citrus skin into the shaker or glass.

I NEVER GO to Atlanta without hitting Holeman & Finch, Linton Hopkins's casually cool, rock-and-roll restaurant with incredible cheeseburgers (they don't come out until ten o'clock) and killer cocktails. This drink comes from Greg Best, their beverage guru, who confesses that the name comes from happy memories of walking down Charleston's King Street with friends, sipping bourbon from hip flasks.

Much like Linton's food, the bar is known for thoughtful recipes that celebrate regional ingredients (like sorghum syrup, a traditional Southern sweetener made from ground sorghum cane), produced in user-friendly, replicable formats. Greg says his favorite bourbons for this recipe are Wathens, for a smooth and elegant finish, or Old Rip Van Winkle ten-year (100 proof) for a spicy assertive flavor. I'll gladly drink either variation.

KING STREET
Derby

1½ ounces small-batch bourbon

1 ounce fresh grapefruit juice, preferably white

½ ounce sorghum syrup (molasses or cane syrup can be used as a substitute)

6 dashes of Regan's Orange Bitters No. 6

Mint sprig

Combine the bourbon, grapefruit juice, sorghum (loosened with ½ tablespoon warm water if exceptionally thick), and bitters in a cocktail shaker with ice. Shake vigorously, strain through a fine sieve into a stemmed cocktail glass, and garnish with the mint sprig.

ONE TIME CHUCK Magill, the dapper general manager of the Capital Hotel in Little Rock, saved my life. I'd taken my family on an ill-fated camping trip to Arkansas, and fled the campgrounds in a thunderstorm to find refuge. We ended up in some sketchy hotel that seemed to be haunted. Finally, after a bizarre night in this place, I gave Chuck a call. I knew him from his time in New Orleans, when he used to frequent Herbsaint.

Chuck is an old-school gentleman of beautiful manners. His shoes are always shined and his bow tie perfectly cinched. He didn't hesitate a second before saying, "You can't stay there. Come here and we'll take care of you." We arrived to a room full of toys for the kids and, best of all, a babysitter so Amanda and I could have a grown-up dinner. And things improved dramatically when we were given this cold, austere cocktail, garnished with a flower blossom.

When it comes to gin, you can use Plymouth, which is excellent for its neutrality, or Hendrick's, which has rose and cucumber notes. The bartender at the Capital thought Tanqueray Rangpur, which is distilled with aromatic Rangpur limes, juniper, bay leaf, ginger, and other botanicals, was the perfect match for floral St. Germain and lemon. Make the effort to seek out grapefruit bitters (the Bitter Truth is a great brand); it's amazing how much even a few drops will elevate a drink.

ST. EDWARDS
No. 1

Combine the gin, St. Germain, lemon juice, and grapefruit bitters in a cocktail shaker with a scoop of ice. Shake vigorously, strain into a coupe glass, and garnish with edible flowers.

2 ounces gin

1 ounce St. Germain elderflower liqueur

½ ounce fresh lemon juice

2 dashes of grapefruit bitters

Edible flower blossoms or a strip of lemon or lime peel, for garnish

THE BAR AT Husk in Charleston is one of the great watering holes in the South, and my favorite one outside of New Orleans because of its bad-ass music and selection of bourbons—which also ticks me off a little because I can't get all of them. My friend Sean Brock, the chef, is passionately devoted to local food; the blackboard above the bar lists how many miles various ingredients on the menu have traveled to get there. Sean and I got to know each other through the Fatback Collective (more on that later; see page 65) and a whole lot of whiskey.

The Copperhead is a perfectly balanced whiskey drink. There's lemon for acid, bitters for a bite, and absinthe for flavor. Sean warns that "the drink will either kill copperheads, cure copperhead bites, or make you see snakes." The wormwood bitters help enhance the absinthe nuance, carrying the flavors through to the back of the palate and extending the complexity of the cocktail.

COPPERHEAD

¼ ounce absinthe

6 dashes of wormwood bitters

Juice of ½ lemon

2½ ounces rye, preferably Rittenhouse

1 strip of lemon peel

Combine the absinthe, bitters, lemon juice, rye, and a handful of ice in a cocktail shaker. Stir with a long spoon to combine and then strain into a rocks glass. Express the lemon peel (see page 24) and add it to the drink. Serve straight up.

AN OLD-FASHIONED IS traditionally made with rye whiskey, but when my friend Julia Reed (more on her in the next chapter) was growing up in Greenville, Mississippi, the house pour was Scotch. The spirit's smoky, peaty notes play surprisingly well in this combination. However, feel free to use your favorite whiskey and you'll end up with one of the best versions of this classic cocktail around.

JULIA REED'S SCOTCH
Old-Fashioned

1 large strip of Meyer lemon or orange peel, scraped to remove as much pith as possible

1 sugar cube, preferably La Perruche brand

3 to 4 dashes of Fee Brothers orange bitters

3 to 4 dashes of Fee Brothers Old Fashion Aromatic Bitters

3 ounces Scotch

1 orange slice

In a rocks glass, muddle the peel, sugar cube, and bitters with 2 teaspoons cold water. Swirl to make sure the liquid coats the glass. Add ice and the Scotch, stir well, and garnish with the orange slice.

UNDER THE GUIDANCE of Bobby Heugel, Anvil Bar & Refuge in Houston has earned a rep as one of the smartest bars in the South. I like it because the drinks have *cojones*. They're strong, boldly flavored, and unabashedly Southern—right up my alley.

According to Bobby, this drink is layered with Southern history. Prior to today's ice machines, the julep was seen as the ultimate symbol of wealth, an ostentatious, heaping pile of ice, which at one point was more expensive by weight than meat or dairy. It's no coincidence that this aristocratic notion is still preserved in the iconic silver cups today.

More easily forgotten, however, is the role that rum played in the South. While we think of bourbon as the quintessential Southern spirit, it was rum that America, including the South, loved first. This cocktail is made with Jamaican rum and Curaçao, which is named for the Antiguan island that bears its name and Curaçao oranges. Light brown demerara sugar adds a richness to cocktails that takes them to another level. Aromatic bitters and plenty of mint leaves temper the booze with a fresh, herbaceous perfume.

ANTIGUAN
Julep

10 fresh mint leaves, plus 2 sprigs for garnish

1 teaspoon Rich Demerara Simple Syrup (recipe follows)

1½ ounces orange liqueur, such as Curaçao

½ ounce overproof Jamaican rum (see Note), preferably Smith & Cross

2 dashes of Angostura bitters

In the base of a julep cup, muddle the mint and syrup. Add the orange liqueur, rum, and bitters. Add crushed ice to the glass and stir. Add more ice, using your hands to form a mound. Press 2 large mint sprigs into the ice.

Rich Demerara Simple Syrup

MAKES ABOUT 1¼ CUPS (10 OUNCES)

1 cup demerara sugar

Combine the sugar and 1 cup water in a small saucepan. Cook, stirring, over medium heat until the sugar fully dissolves. Remove from the heat and let cool to room temperature. Store in a sealed container in the refrigerator for several months.

NOTE: Most rum available in the United States is 80 to 100 proof (40 to 50 percent alcohol by volume). Rums that contain higher concentrations of alcohol are often labeled as "overproof." These rums tend to be more popular in the Caribbean Islands, where locals prefer a stronger drink. They're also used in recipes that call for rum to be ignited (flambé).

THIS DRINK IS from Bouligny Tavern, my friend John Harris's elegant bar housed in a historic cottage on Magazine Street, next to his excellent restaurant Lilette in New Orleans. John has done a killer job representing his Sinatra-era style into what has instantly become a classic drink destination. And best of all, the music is all played on albums—nice touch, John.

According to Cary Palmer, the general manager, this is a wintry cocktail made with local ingredients like Louisiana honey, coffee bitters, and pecans. This drink ends up a tan milky color (like swamp water from the Atchafalaya Basin), and it's rich and strong. Even though it's iced, it has a definite warming effect that would certainly make a frigid deer stand more comfortable.

DEER STAND
Old-Fashioned

½ ounce Honey Syrup (recipe follows)

3 pecan halves, toasted (see page 230)

2 ounces bourbon, preferably Buffalo Trace

3 drops Bittermens New Orleans Coffee Bitters

1 strip of orange peel

In a mixing glass, muddle the honey syrup and pecans. Add the bourbon and bitters, and swirl to mix. Strain the mixture through a fine sieve into an old-fashioned glass filled with ice. Express the oil from the orange strip into the glass and wipe the rim of the glass with the twist.

Honey Syrup

MAKES ABOUT ½ CUP (2 OUNCES)

2 tablespoons honey

Heat the honey with 2 tablespoons water in a small skillet. Simmer briefly until thickened and then let cool.

Old-School Southern COCKTAIL PARTIES

Spicy Roasted Peanuts 36

FANCY SPICED PECANS 38

Crab Louis with Toast Points 39

URUGUAYAN SPICY BAKED CHEESE 40

Creamy Onion Dip 43

CHICKEN LIVER PÂTÉ 44

Sweet and Sour Onion Jam 46

SOUTHERN BRUSCHETTA WITH BACON AND TOMATO 47

Cajun-Spiced Soda Crackers 48

SPICY CHEDDAR CRACKERS 49

Parmesan Bacon Gougères 51

SHRIMP RÉMOULADE 52

Blue Crab Beignets with White Rémoulade Sauce 54

BLACK PEPPER BISCUITS WITH COUNTRY HAM AND HOT MUSTARD SAUCE 56

Beef Tenderloin and Yeast Rolls with Horseradish Cream Sauce 58

There were white taper candles and fresh flowers, paper doilies, and parsley garnishes. The men wore bow ties and the women smelled like Shalimar and cigarettes. There was an unabashed consumption of mayonnaise, cream cheese, and Ritz crackers. Thrown in lush gardens and ornate parlors and on back porches and grand estates, old-school Southern cocktail parties were (and still are) the pressed linen grandeur of the old South.

No one embodies the decadent spirit of these affairs more than my friend Julia Reed. As a journalist, she's spent most of her adult life writing (for *Vogue* and *The New York Times*, among other publications) about eating and drinking in the South. She chronicles the region's ironies and its blending of high–low culture (especially when it comes to food) better than anyone. When she was growing up in Greenville, Mississippi, her mother would whip together impromptu parties for visiting dignitaries on a day's notice. Her father, a Republican Party strategist, would bring home some bigwig, like Ronald Reagan, Robert Novak, or William F. Buckley, Jr.

Here's the funny thing: Most Southern men feel as at home in a grungy hunting camp as they do at a black-tie gala: That's just part of the culture. And yet there's a funny feeling that comes from dressing up and going to a formal party, not unlike playing dress-up as kid. You get to be a different character for a night, and have conversations that you normally wouldn't. Then once the bourbon or Scotch has been flowing for a bit, you inevitably go from pretend socialite to college student, playing "House of the Rising Sun" (with me on guitar and John, Julia's husband, on piano) and smoking cigarettes. There's always a tipping point, a graceful exit of formality before the booze kicks in and leads to long conversations where you make lasting connections with the other guests.

I've had several such nights at Julia's, so it seemed only appropriate to shoot this chapter in her beautiful home in the Garden District.

When it comes to entertaining, this chapter provides a feast of options for a party of finger foods, a holiday buffet, or just a few small plates to make a fantastic meal. For me, the flavors are steeped in memories, and the recipes are a good excuse to get cleaned up, gather in a beautiful space with friends, and eat and drink well.

IN THE LATE summer, Burris Market in Loxley, Alabama, has locally grown peanuts in every form imaginable: raw in the shell, raw out of the shell, roasted in and out of the shell, and boiled in Cajun spice. Along the rural roadsides, you can find farmers selling bags of boiled peanuts out of the back of their trucks, as well as Styrofoam cups of just-cooked batches, still moist from their salty bath. Hit your turn signal because these are not your ballpark-variety peanuts. Roasting fresh peanuts that have been seasoned with salt and red spices creates an addictive party snack—and the perfect sidekick to ice-cold beer.

These cooking instructions are based on small peanuts; for a larger variety you may want to increase the cooking time by an additional 20 to 30 minutes. Watch the coloring closely toward the end—when fully roasted, the peanuts should be lightly tanned but not brown, or they'll taste bitter.

SPICY ROASTED
Peanuts

MAKES 1 POUND

1 pound fresh, unroasted, peeled small peanuts

2 teaspoons peanut or vegetable oil

2 tablespoons unsalted butter

1 tablespoon sugar

2 teaspoons kosher salt, plus more to taste

½ teaspoon paprika

½ teaspoon cayenne

Heat the oven to 300°F.

Put the peanuts on a rimmed baking sheet, drizzle with the peanut oil, and toss until evenly coated. Roast, stirring every 20 minutes or so, until the nuts are fragrant and lightly tanned (but not brown), about 1 hour and 15 minutes.

Toward the end of roasting time, melt the butter in a medium skillet. Add the sugar, salt, paprika, and cayenne and cook, stirring, for a few minutes without browning the butter, to warm the spices. Using a rubber spatula, transfer the mixture to a large mixing bowl.

When the nuts are done, remove from the heat, cool slightly, and transfer to the bowl. Toss with the butter mixture for at least a minute to ensure that the spices are evenly distributed. Finish with a few pinches of salt (adding more or less to taste). Allow the peanuts to cool completely before serving—freshly roasted peanuts will remain mealy and soft until they are cooled, when they'll regain their crunchy texture.

I CAN'T FATHOM that the entire world wouldn't want spicy peanuts all the time, but Julia Reed insists that they are not appropriate at cocktail parties, where pecans—the classier nut—rule. For me, pecans signal the beginning of fall. Once they start clattering down roofs and appearing at roadside stands, the hot weather in Louisiana is gone, for a few months anyhow. Large, freshly harvested pecans are indeed a luxury. Their rich flavor doesn't need much embellishment—but a little butter, Worcestershire, salt, and heat make them irresistible.

FANCY SPICED
Pecans

MAKES 1 POUND

1 pound large shelled pecans

4 tablespoons (½ stick) unsalted butter, melted

2 tablespoons Worcestershire sauce

2 teaspoons kosher salt

½ teaspoon cayenne

Heat the oven to 400°F.

Toss the pecans, butter, Worcestershire, salt, and cayenne together in a large bowl. Transfer to a rimmed baking sheet and bake for 30 minutes.

Reduce the oven temperature to 275°F and bake the pecans, stirring every 15 minutes or so, until fragrant and lightly toasted, an additional 30 minutes. Allow the nuts to cool completely before serving.

ACCORDING TO JULIA, if you're going to serve this at a dinner party, it should look opulent and grand, so make it a big pile of it. There are simpler ways to prepare this sauce (that involve commercial chile sauce), but I prefer to impart a roasted green chile flavor from a poblano and smokiness from chipotle chiles.

CRAB LOUIS
with Toast Points

SERVES 12 TO 15

4 pounds jumbo lump crabmeat

1 poblano pepper

2 red jalapeños

1 medium tomato

2 garlic cloves, smashed and peeled

2 chipotle chiles packed in adobo sauce

½ small onion, diced

2 teaspoons Worcestershire sauce

1 tablespoon fresh lemon juice

1 tablespoon sugar

1 teaspoon hot sauce

1½ cups mayonnaise

1 head iceberg lettuce, cored and thinly sliced

8 slices of white bread, lightly toasted, crusts trimmed, each sliced into 4 triangles

Pick and clean the crabmeat at least twice, then cover, and refrigerate until needed.

Heat the oven to 500°F.

Roast the poblano and jalapeños on a baking sheet until the skins have blackened and the peppers are soft and wrinkled, about 15 minutes. Put the peppers in a mixing bowl and cover with plastic wrap for 10 minutes.

Peel the skin from the peppers and then stem and seed them.

Cut the tomato in half and roast in a small cast-iron skillet in the oven until cooked down and a little paste-like, about 6 minutes. Add the garlic and roast for an additional 4 minutes.

Combine the peppers, tomato and garlic, chipotles, onion, Worcestershire, lemon juice, sugar, and hot sauce in a food processor and process to a fine puree. Transfer the chile mixture to a large bowl, add the mayonnaise, and combine. (You should have about 3 cups sauce.) Chill the mixture in the fridge for at least 30 minutes.

Gently fold about ⅓ cup of the sauce into the crabmeat. Taste and add more as desired. Serve the dressed crab atop the iceberg lettuce, with the toast points on the side. (Use leftover sauce as a dressing for additional crab, or for chicken or shrimp salad; it will keep in the fridge for 2 weeks.)

WHEN IT COMES to cocktail party fare, never underestimate the power of hot cheese.

The menus I saw in Uruguay listed this dish as simply "Provolone," but I knew what that meant: a hot, melty, salty, gooey mess of cheese. A square or round of provolone yields great results, but I've also made this recipe with local farmer Bill Ryal's goat cheddar; it's a delicious option. This is a great dish to pull out of the oven before dinner, while everyone is standing around the kitchen counter watching you cook. It gets a lot of "Wow!" and "Oh my god!" to which you reply, "Yeah, I know, right?" You can serve the warm cheese with slices of good bread, although honestly you don't need anything but a fork.

URUGUAYAN
Spicy Baked Cheese

SERVES 4 TO 6 AS AN APPETIZER

½ pound semihard cheese with flat sides, such as provolone, in a square or round

1 tablespoon olive oil

1 teaspoon dried oregano

½ teaspoon kosher salt

⅛ teaspoon red pepper flakes

2 tablespoons best-quality extra-virgin olive oil

1 lemon wedge

Heat the oven to 450°F.

Heat a cast-iron skillet over medium-high heat. Lightly coat the cheese with the olive oil and put it in the hot skillet (it is not necessary to oil the skillet because the cheese is coated with oil). Cook until a golden crust forms on the bottom, 3 to 4 minutes. Carefully flip the cheese over (try to lift the cheese up with the spatula as you slide it underneath, so you don't mess up the nice crust you just created).

At this point the cheese should still be slightly firm. Put the skillet in the oven until the cheese softens and begins to melt but doesn't completely lose its shape, about 1 minute. (Note: If the cheese is already good and melted after you sear it on one side, you can skip this step entirely.)

Put the cheese on a serving platter and sprinkle the oregano, salt, and red pepper flakes over the top. Just before serving, drizzle with the extra-virgin olive oil and some fresh lemon juice.

WHEN I WAS growing up, my mother taught my sister and me how to play cards—poker, blackjack, and spades, to name a few games. An essential part of the table setup was a bowl of creamy onion dip and potato chips. These days, whenever I find myself at a party with onion dip I always think about those card games and how great it was to spend time with my family—yet another example of how so many foods carry such power of place and time.

This is my updated version, which relies on sweet sautéed onions and a rich sour cream–mascarpone base. It's delicious served with potato chips or Spicy Cheddar Crackers (page 49). When we prepared this dip for a party at Julia Reed's house, we discovered that a splash of Armagnac deepens the flavors in a delicious way (for that matter, a splash of Armagnac improves just about anything). In fact, Julia splashed in more every time she passed through the kitchen. Fine Armagnac is expensive—feel free to use Cognac or brandy as a replacement.

CREAMY

Onion Dip

SERVES 4 TO 6

2 tablespoons olive oil

2 large sweet onions, diced small

2 tablespoons chopped fresh thyme

1 tablespoon plus 1 teaspoon kosher salt

2 teaspoons cayenne

1½ teaspoons black pepper

1 teaspoon garlic powder

1 cup sour cream

¾ cup mayonnaise

½ cup mascarpone

1 bunch scallions, thinly sliced

1 tablespoon fresh lemon juice

1 tablespoon Armagnac, Cognac, or brandy, plus more to taste

Heat the oil in a large skillet over medium heat and swirl to coat. Add the onions and sauté, stirring, until they begin to release their water, about 5 minutes. Reduce the heat to low and sauté until the onions are very soft but not brown, about 30 minutes.

Add the thyme, salt, cayenne, black pepper, and garlic powder and cook, stirring, for an additional 3 minutes to heat the spices. Remove from the heat, transfer the onion mixture to a bowl, and cool completely (you can chill the mixture in the fridge to speed up this process). Add the sour cream, mayonnaise, mascarpone, scallions, lemon juice, and Armagnac and stir until combined. Taste for seasonings and adjust the flavors as desired.

Refrigerate the mixture for at least 1 hour and up to 8 hours before serving to allow the flavors to develop.

I WOULD NOT recommend making this for your child's birthday party; it probably wouldn't go over too well. I would, however, make it for any gathering where Champagne is being poured. The accompaniments are key to serving a good pâté. Even though I like this on its own, I would definitely put out that great jar of mustard you've been saving, or serve it along with something sweet and sour, like Sweet and Sour Onion Jam (page 46), and some crusty bread or a pile of toast points.

Note that you'll want to prepare this the day before you serve it. Chilling the pâté overnight allows the flavors to develop and the textures to firm up.

CHICKEN LIVER
Pâté

MAKES ONE 2½-CUP CROCK OR TERRINE

1 pound chicken livers
½ pound bacon, diced
1 cup thinly sliced shallots
1 teaspoon minced garlic
¼ cup brandy
2 teaspoons chopped fresh thyme
1 teaspoon Pâté Spice (recipe follows)
2 teaspoons kosher salt
⅛ teaspoon curing salt (see Note)
⅛ teaspoon cayenne
½ cup heavy cream
2 large egg yolks

Preheat the oven to 300°F.

Rinse the chicken livers and drain them in a colander; pat dry with paper towels.

Cook the bacon in a large skillet over medium heat until rendered but not crispy, about 5 minutes. Add the shallots and garlic and cook until softened, about 2 minutes. Remove from the heat and pour in the brandy. Return to medium heat, add the thyme and spice mix, and simmer, stirring, until the pan is almost dry. Remove from the heat and allow the mixture to cool completely.

Combine the livers, bacon mixture, kosher salt, curing salt, cayenne, cream, and egg yolks in a food processor and puree until smooth. Pour the mixture into a 2½-cup crock or terrine mold. Put the dish in a cake pan and add enough water to come halfway up the sides. Bake until the internal temperature reaches 155°F, about 1 hour and 10 minutes. Remove from the oven and cool the loaf pan in an ice bath before refrigerating overnight.

Serve the pâté straight from the crock, alongside the condiments.

NOTE: Curing salt, typically a blend of table salt and sodium nitrate, is used when curing and pickling meats and making sausage because it prevents or slows the spoilage of these foods. It is also called "pink salt" because it's dyed pink to blend better with meat—and so you don't confuse it with table salt.

Pâté Spice

MAKES 1 TABLESPOON

¾ teaspoon ground white
    pepper
½ teaspoon ground ginger
½ teaspoon ground fennel
    seed
½ teaspoon ground coriander
¼ teaspoon ground cinnamon
¼ teaspoon ground cloves
¼ teaspoon ground nutmeg

Combine all the ingredients in a
container with a lid, cover, and
store in a cool, dark place for
up to 6 months.

THIS RICH, FULL-FLAVORED condiment is sweet from sautéed shallots and sour from a nice amount of vinegar. It's the perfect condiment for Chicken Liver Pâté (page 44), but it's also good on a sandwich with thinly sliced roast pork and a mild white cheese. You can serve this jam immediately, but it's even better after being refrigerated overnight, to allow the flavors to meld.

SWEET AND SOUR
Onion Jam

MAKES ABOUT 1½ CUPS

4 cups coarsely chopped shallots (or red or yellow onions)

½ cup sugar

1½ cups red wine vinegar

1 teaspoon kosher salt

1 (4-inch) rosemary sprig

1 dried criola sella chile or chile de árbol

Combine all the ingredients in a small, heavy-bottomed saucepan and cook over very low heat, stirring occasionally, for about 2¼ hours, or until the onions are soft and the mixture is thick, like marmalade. Add small amounts of water as needed to provide enough moisture to fully cook the onions.

Remove from the heat and let cool. For the best flavor, refrigerate the jam overnight before serving (it will keep for several weeks). For the deepest flavor, leave the rosemary and chile stem in the jam during storage, but remove them before serving.

I MADE THESE toasts recently for my wife Amanda's birthday party, and of all the elaborate hors d'oeuvres that I prepared that day, these were all anyone could talk about. They are ridiculously simple, but they rely on one of the most brilliant combinations that we humans have discovered. How can you top salty bacon, ripe tomatoes, and one of my all-time favorite ingredients, mayonnaise?

SOUTHERN BRUSCHETTA
with Bacon and Tomato

MAKES 16 TOASTS

6 ounces sliced bacon

4 slices white bread, crusts trimmed

1 large, perfectly ripe tomato, cut into small dice

1 tablespoon extra-virgin olive oil

2 teaspoons sherry wine vinegar

1 tablespoon minced scallion

2 basil leaves, thinly sliced

¼ teaspoon kosher salt

⅛ teaspoon black pepper

About 2 tablespoons mayonnaise

Heat the oven to 325°F.

Put the bacon strips between two sheets of parchment paper on a rimmed baking sheet. Top with another baking sheet (this will keep the bacon flat and prevent the edges from curling up, which will make for nicer-looking bruschetta). Cook until the bacon is crisp but not burned, about 15 minutes. Transfer the bacon to a plate lined with paper towels to cool. (Alternatively, you can pan fry the bacon in a skillet until crisp.)

While the bacon is cooking, toast the white bread and cut each piece into 4 equal squares. Combine the tomato with the olive oil, vinegar, scallions, basil, salt, and pepper.

Cut the bacon into squares to fit the toast.

To serve, spread about ½ teaspoon mayonnaise on each toast square, spoon on about a tablespoon of the tomato mixture, and top with a square of bacon.

THESE RICH AND spicy crackers are great with Creamy Onion Dip (page 43), Smoked Mullet Dip (page 159), or Crab Louis (page 39). They're also the perfect partner for a bowl of creamy oyster stew or a cheese board.

When it comes to making your own crackers, a few tricks will ensure perfect results. Chilling the dough before rolling it out makes the process much easier. Make sure you lightly flour your work surface *and* rolling pin before rolling out the dough. Remember that the crackers will be broken into irregular shards, so don't sweat rolling them into a perfect shape. Be sure to bake them to a golden brown color; underbaked crackers won't have a crisp texture. Wait until the crackers are completely cool before you break them into pieces (if they don't seem crisp enough, you can always return them to the oven for an additional 5 minutes).

CAJUN-SPICED
Soda Crackers

MAKES ABOUT 4 DOZEN

¾ cup rendered lard, cold
4 cups all-purpose flour
1½ teaspoons kosher salt
1 teaspoon baking powder
½ teaspoon black pepper
½ teaspoon garlic powder
½ teaspoon onion powder
½ teaspoon dried thyme
¼ teaspoon cayenne
¼ teaspoon celery seed
1⅓ cups whole milk

In the bowl of an electric mixer fitted with a dough hook, combine the lard, flour, salt, baking powder, black pepper, garlic and onion powders, thyme, cayenne, and celery seed. With the mixer running on low speed, add the milk and mix until incorporated. Increase the speed to medium and mix for 8 minutes, to pull the dough together. Wrap the dough in plastic and refrigerate for at least 1 hour and up to 3 days (or freeze for up to 1 month).

When you're ready to bake, adjust an oven rack to the middle position and heat the oven to 350°F. Line a rimmed baking sheet with parchment paper.

Unwrap the dough and divide it into quarters. Wrap three of the quarters in plastic and return to the fridge. With a lightly floured rolling pin, roll out one section of the dough on a lightly floured surface to the desired thickness; for a thin cracker, the dough should be less than ¼ inch thick. Drape the dough over the rolling pin and transfer it to the prepared baking sheet (use your fingers to stretch and spread it into place, as needed). Bake until golden brown, 10 to 15 minutes; allow the crackers to cool on the baking sheet. Repeat with the remaining quarters of dough, using a completely cool sheet each time.

Once the crackers have cooled to room temperature, break into pieces (irregular shards look the best; you'll get about 12 per square), and serve. Stored in an airtight container, the crackers will last 1 week.

ALTHOUGH THESE SPICY, rich crackers are a great base for toppings like pimento cheese and Creamy Onion Dip (page 43), they really are perfect all by themselves. I recommend placing a platter of them on the table, alongside a few other appetizers, but be prepared to replenish the supply because they will go fast.

It's important to keep everything cold for this recipe, so the dough will be easier to work with and the crackers will be crisp and light.

SPICY CHEDDAR
Crackers

MAKES ABOUT 4 DOZEN

4 tablespoons (½ stick) unsalted butter, cold

¼ cup rendered bacon fat, cold

1 tablespoon balsamic vinegar

1 cup (loosely packed) freshly grated Parmesan cheese

1 cup grated Cheddar cheese

2½ cups all-purpose flour

1½ teaspoons kosher salt

½ teaspoon baking powder

¾ to 1 teaspoon cayenne, to taste

½ teaspoon black pepper

2 tablespoons honey

Cut the butter into ½-inch cubes; combine with the bacon fat and chill for 30 minutes. Combine the vinegar and ¼ cup plus 3 tablespoons cold water and refrigerate for 30 minutes. Combine the cheeses and chill in the refrigerator.

Combine the flour, salt, baking powder, cayenne, and black pepper and the cold cheese in the bowl of a food processor and pulse until combined. Add the butter and bacon fat and pulse until just incorporated.

With the processor running, slowly add the honey and the water-vinegar mixture to pull the dough together. Wrap the dough in plastic and refrigerate for at least 1 hour or up to 3 days (or freeze for up to 1 month).

When you're ready to bake, adjust an oven rack to the middle position and heat the oven to 350°F. Line a rimmed baking sheet with parchment paper.

Unwrap the dough and divide it into quarters. Wrap three of the quarters in plastic and return to the fridge. With a lightly floured rolling pin, roll out one section of the dough on a lightly floured surface to the desired thickness; for a thin cracker, the dough should be less than ¼ inch thick. Drape the dough over the rolling pin and transfer it to the prepared baking sheet (use your fingers to stretch and spread it into place, as needed). Bake until golden brown, 10 to 15 minutes; allow the crackers to cool on the baking sheet. Repeat with the remaining quarters of dough, using a completely cool baking sheet each time.

Once the crackers have cooled to room temperature, break into pieces (irregular chards look the best; you'll get about 12 per square), and serve. Stored in an airtight container, the crackers will last 1 week.

WITH A CRACKLY shell and a light, pillowy middle, gougères, also called cheese puffs, are one of the most perfect foods to pop in your mouth between sips of your favorite adult beverage (they're delicious with Champagne). The Parmesan and bacon add a rich, savory flavor that makes them difficult to stop eating.

PARMESAN BACON
Gougères

MAKES 2 DOZEN

4 strips of thick-sliced bacon

½ cup whole milk

4 tablespoons (½ stick) unsalted butter

1 teaspoon kosher salt

1 teaspoon onion powder

½ teaspoon sugar

⅛ teaspoon cayenne

1¼ cups bread flour, sifted

3 large eggs

1¼ cups freshly grated Parmesan cheese

Heat the oven to 425°F. Line 2 baking sheets with parchment paper.

Cook the bacon in a large skillet over medium-low heat until crisp but not too dark. Transfer the bacon to a plate lined with paper towels, and reserve ¼ cup of the rendered fat. When the bacon is cool, chop to make ½ cup.

Bring the milk, ½ cup water, the butter, and the reserved bacon fat to a simmer in a medium saucepan over medium heat. Stir in the salt, onion powder, sugar, and cayenne. Add the flour and, using a wooden spoon, stir very quickly in one direction. The flour will quickly absorb the liquid and form a dough. Continue stirring to cook the flour (and remove its "raw" taste) and simmer off more of the moisture until the dough pulls away from the sides of the saucepan, an additional minute or two.

Transfer the dough to the bowl of an electric mixer fitted with the paddle attachment.

Add the eggs one at a time, mixing on medium speed until each is incorporated into the dough, which will change from shiny to sticky as the eggs are worked in. On low speed, stir in 1 cup of the Parmesan and the bacon until just combined.

Using a small ice cream scoop (about 2 inches in diameter), scoop the dough onto the prepared baking sheets. Top the gougères with an equal amount of the remaining ¼ cup Parmesan.

Bake until puffed and golden, 20 to 25 minutes. Serve warm.

WHEN IT COMES to the best way to enjoy cold shrimp, the choice is definitely between spicy boiled shrimp and those same shrimp served with a creamy, zippy rémoulade sauce over some ice-cold, crispy iceberg lettuce. I guess, truth be told, it depends on whether I'm going to be standing or sitting (with a knife and fork) to eat!

SHRIMP
Rémoulade

**SERVES 4 TO 6 AS A
SNACK OR LIGHT MEAL**

1 cup kosher salt

1 tablespoon cayenne

10 bay leaves

2 lemons, sliced

2 pounds medium-large shrimp
  in the shell

1 cup Sauce Rémoulade
  (recipe follows)

½ head iceberg lettuce,
  thinly sliced

Combine the salt, cayenne, bay leaves, and lemon slices in a large pot with 1 gallon water and bring to a rolling boil over high heat. Add the shrimp and cook until the shrimp are bright pink and just cooked through, 3 to 3½ minutes. Immediately pour 2 gallons of ice into the pot and allow the shrimp to cool completely in the poaching liquid (this should take 5 to 10 minutes). Peel.

Toss the peeled shrimp with the sauce and serve over the lettuce.

Sauce Rémoulade

MAKES 1½ CUPS

You'll need only a portion of this recipe for 2 pounds of shrimp. The remainder will keep in the fridge for two to three days, and will make a quick meal when tossed with more shrimp or crab, or slathered on a fried fish sandwich.

¼ cup grated yellow onion

1 cup mayonnaise

2 tablespoons whole-grain mustard

2 tablespoons chopped fresh parsley

2 tablespoons chopped fresh tarragon or chervil

2 tablespoons prepared horseradish

¼ teaspoon cayenne

¼ teaspoon paprika

Grated zest and juice of 2 lemons

1 teaspoon kosher salt

Use a rubber spatula to combine all ingredients in a mixing bowl. Refrigerate for at least 1 hour.

THE GREAT THING about blue crab is that it is found across the Gulf South, from Texas to Maryland. As a boy I remember pulling blue crabs out of the waters and canals and being amazed at the beautiful deep, saturated color of their shells.

These crispy one-bite beignets deliver a sweet, luxurious mouthful of crab. When serving them for a crowd, I advise spacing them out (they keep well in a low oven) between other hors d'oeuvres, because these are always the first to disappear.

This recipe calls for an easy, rustic method of spooning the batter directly into the hot oil. For a fancier presentation (and a crispier crust) you can shape the chilled beignet batter into $1\frac{1}{2}$-inch balls and then lightly roll the balls in additional panko crumbs before frying. These beignets are delicious served on their own, and even more decadent when dipped in creamy white rémoulade. For an old-school presentation, serve on a plate covered with paper doilies and garnished with sprigs of parsley.

BLUE CRAB BEIGNETS
with White Rémoulade Sauce

MAKES ABOUT 16 BEIGNETS

1 pound blue crab meat
2 large eggs
1 cup mayonnaise
2 tablespoons Creole mustard
2 teaspoons fresh lemon juice
¼ cup thinly sliced scallions
¼ cup finely diced red onion
1½ teaspoons kosher salt
½ teaspoon black pepper
Pinch of cayenne
1 cup panko (Japanese bread crumbs)
Canola oil, for frying
1 cup White Rémoulade Sauce (recipe follows)

Put the crabmeat in a bowl and use your hands to pick the meat free of any shells. Do this at least twice.

In a medium bowl, whisk the eggs until they're light and foamy and then whisk in the mayonnaise and mustard. Use a wooden spoon to stir in the lemon juice, scallions, red onion, salt, black pepper, and cayenne. Fold in the panko and then gently fold in the crabmeat so it doesn't get broken up from too much mixing. The batter should be just thick enough to barely hold together when frying. Refrigerate for at least 1 hour to help it firm up further.

In a large, deep skillet or pot, heat 2 inches of canola oil to 350°F.

Using 2 table spoons (the kind you eat with, not measure with), drop a few spoonfuls of the crab mixture at a time into the oil and fry until a nice golden brown color forms on the outside, 1 to 2 minutes. Use a slotted spoon to transfer the beignets to a plate lined with paper towels. Repeat with the remaining batter, frying in batches so as not to crowd the pan. You can keep the cooked beignets warm in a 200°F oven, if desired.

White Rémoulade Sauce

MAKES 1 GENEROUS CUP

¼ cup minced yellow onion

¼ cup thinly sliced scallions

Grated zest and juice of
½ lemon

⅛ teaspoon Worcestershire
sauce

1 cup mayonnaise

Combine all the ingredients
in a bowl and chill for at least
30 minutes or up to 8 hours
to allow the flavors to develop
before serving.

THE STAR ON any Southern party table is a pedestal of sliced salt-cured country ham, ready to be eaten with buttery biscuits.

Curing country hams properly is a time-honored process, and one of the oldest methods of food preservation in the South. Seasonings like salt and brown sugar are rubbed into the meat by hand, and then the ham is rinsed, hung, and smoked over a hickory wood fire. The smoke infuses the ham with a deep, complex flavor. After twelve to eighteen months of aging, the result is an intense concentration of salty goodness that rivals the aged hams from Italy and Spain.

What I like about this biscuit recipe is how the shortening is incorporated into the dough. Instead of being cut into the flour, as usual, it's added to the dough toward the end of mixing, which makes the dough messier to work with but results in a flakier biscuit.

When Julia Reed was growing up, the ham and biscuits were always joined by her mom's delicious hot mustard sauce. These are perfect for brunch, picnics, and lunch boxes, and will likely steal the show on a festive table of party foods.

BLACK PEPPER BISCUITS
with Country Ham and Hot Mustard Sauce

SERVES 10 TO 12

8 tablespoons (1 stick) unsalted butter, cold, plus more for the baking sheet

4½ cups all-purpose flour

2 tablespoons baking powder

2 teaspoons kosher salt

2 teaspoons sugar

1 teaspoon black pepper

1½ cups buttermilk

¾ cup vegetable shortening

Hot Mustard Sauce (recipe follows)

8 ounces thinly sliced country ham

Heat the oven to 400°F. Butter a baking sheet.

Combine 4 cups of the flour, the baking powder, salt, sugar, and pepper in a large mixing bowl. Cut 6 tablespoons of the butter into slices and use your fingertips to work the butter into the flour mixture until it is pebbly and coarse. Make a well in the center of the flour mixture, pour in the buttermilk, and combine with a fork—this is going to be messy. Form the dough into a wet, sticky ball and work the shortening into the dough by hand. Use the remaining ½ cup flour to coat your hands and work surface while you work with the dough. Turn the dough onto a lightly floured work surface and shape it into a ¾-inch-thick rectangle. Fold the dough over itself, like you're folding a sheet of paper to insert into an envelope, roll out ¾ inch thick, and repeat this process three times. This will develop flaky layers.

Use a knife to cut the dough into 2- to 3-inch-wide squares, put the biscuits on the baking sheet (so they are not touching), and bake until light golden brown on top, 25 to 30 minutes. Let cool on wire racks, then split, and serve with mustard sauce and ham.

Hot Mustard Sauce

MAKES ¾ CUP

This sauce keeps well for weeks, so after the ham fest you'll have an awesome sandwich condiment that will dramatically improve your lunch hour.

½ cup Coleman's dry mustard
½ cup cider vinegar
½ cup sugar
1 large egg, beaten well
½ teaspoon kosher salt

Combine the mustard and vinegar in a stainless steel bowl. Cover and macerate overnight.

Put the mustard mixture in the top of a double boiler over gently simmering water. Add the sugar, egg, and salt and whisk constantly until the mixture thickens, about 3 minutes. Remove from the heat. The mixture will be like a thick soup, but it will thicken considerably when refrigerated. Let cool and then refrigerate.

My Favorite COUNTRY HAMS

These hams are all available via mail order, and completely worth the splurge for a party or holiday table:

Benton's Smoky Mountain Country Hams,
bentonscountryhams2.com

S. Wallace Edwards & Sons,
virginiatraditions.com

Broadbent's,
broadbenthams.com

Colonel Bill Newsom's Hams,
newsomscountryham.com

Father's Country Hams,
fatherscountryhams.com

WHAT COULD BE more delicious than beef, rubbed with herbs and roasted on thick slabs of onion, sliced thin and served on a fresh yeast roll with creamy horseradish sauce? Like mounds of crab Louis and asparagus spears, roasted beef tenderloin is an iconic luxury item on any party table. If you're lucky enough to have leftovers, you'll be in sandwich heaven the next day.

The yeast roll recipe makes more than you'll need for one tenderloin, but the rolls freeze beautifully, so you'll be armed for lunch the next time you make a shrimp or chicken salad or have leftover Tupelo Honey–Glazed Ham (page 103).

BEEF TENDERLOIN *and* YEAST ROLLS
with Horseradish Cream Sauce

SERVES 18 TO 20

1 (5- to 7-pound) beef tenderloin, trimmed and cleaned

2 tablespoons kosher salt

2 tablespoons chopped fresh thyme

2 teaspoons black pepper

1 large onion, sliced into ½-inch rings

Horseradish Cream Sauce (recipe follows)

Sherry Prewitt's Yeast Rolls (recipe follows)

An hour before cooking the tenderloin, take it out of the fridge and allow the meat to come to room temperature.

Heat the oven to 500°F.

Massage the meat with the salt, thyme, and pepper. Line the bottom of a roasting pan with the onion slices and put the meat on top. Roast until the beef has a golden brown exterior and the onion begins to sizzle in the fat, about 15 minutes.

Remove the pan from the oven and reduce the oven temperature to 300°F. Return the tenderloin to the oven until it reaches an internal temperature of 125°F, about 15 minutes more.

Tent the meat loosely with foil and let it rest for 20 minutes. Thinly slice the beef and serve with the sauce and yeast rolls.

Horseradish Cream Sauce

MAKES ABOUT 2½ CUPS

2 cups sour cream

½ cup prepared horseradish

¼ cup heavy cream

2 tablespoons Dijon mustard

2 tablespoons fresh lemon juice

2 teaspoons sugar

1 teaspoon Worcestershire sauce

Pinch each of kosher salt and black pepper

Combine all of the ingredients in a medium bowl. Refrigerate for at least 1 hour and up to 8 hours before serving.

Sherry Prewitt's Yeast Rolls

MAKES ABOUT 3 DOZEN ROLLS

These tender, split-and-fold style rolls (also called refrigerator rolls or pocket rolls) come from the mother of Ryan Prewitt, a partner in our restaurant group; she makes them every Thanksgiving and Christmas.

½ cup vegetable shortening
Scant ¼ cup sugar
¾ teaspoon kosher salt
1 package active dry yeast
1 large egg
3 cups all-purpose flour
4 tablespoons (½ stick) unsalted butter, melted

In a large mixing bowl, combine the shortening, sugar, salt, and ½ cup boiling water. Stir until mixed and set aside to cool.

In a small bowl, mix the yeast with ¼ cup warm water.

In a separate bowl, beat the egg with ¼ cup water and then stir into the yeast mixture.

When the shortening mixture is lukewarm, use a fork to stir in the egg mixture. Stir in the flour, 1 cup at a time, mixing until just blended. Cover and set aside until doubled in size, several hours, or refrigerate overnight.

When you're ready to prepare the rolls, divide the dough in half and set one half aside. On a lightly floured surface, knead the other half several times. With a rolling pin, flatten to a ½-inch thickness and cut with a 3-inch biscuit cutter.

Dip each piece in melted butter and fold over to make the pocket rolls. Put on a baking sheet 3 inches apart and cover with a damp cloth or paper towel. Allow to rise in a warm spot until doubled in size, 2 to 3 hours.

Heat the oven to 400°F.

Bake the rolls until light golden, about 12 minutes. Put the baking sheet on a cooling rack and allow the rolls to cool completely.

NOTE: The baked rolls may be frozen until needed. Make sure they are completely cool before freezing them in a tightly sealed freezer bag. You can thaw the rolls at room temperature or remove the frozen rolls from the freezer bag, wrap in aluminum foil, and reheat at 350°F, until just warmed through, about 10 minutes.

Cook It
OUTSIDE

Chicken Chivito Sandwich with
Ham and Olive Spread 69

GRILLED CHICKEN ON A
STICK WITH ALABAMA WHITE
BARBECUE SAUCE 70

Grilled Chicken Breasts with
Lemon-Olive Vinaigrette 72

SMOKED CHICKEN THIGHS 73

Smoked Duck with Aromatic Salt 74

SPICY GRILLED QUAIL WITH
GRILLED PEACHES 75

Mamou Grilled Pork
Steak Sandwich 76

GRILLED PORK TENDERLOINS
WITH ARUGULA AND
PARMESAN 78

Grilled Pork Chops with Sweet and
Sour Dried Fruit 79

GRILLED HAM STEAK WITH
CHARRED BLOOD ORANGES 81

Grilled Boneless Lamb Saddle 83

ROAST LEG OF LAMB WITH
TEXAS CAMPFIRE DRY RUB 84

Beer-Smoked Beef Short Ribs 88

Barbecue purists, myself included, will tell you that the only *real* barbecue is meat cooked over wood, not charcoal, and definitely not gas—ever. In the South that's just not considered barbecue. There is something that feels completely primitive about cooking over fire. Just ask the thousands of people who gather in May to slow-smoke meats in Memphis, a mecca for barbecue enthusiasts from all over the country. I've never seen anything like it—imagine every and any cut of pork slow-cooked every way possible on the banks of the Mississippi.

A few years ago, my friend Nick Pihakis (a partner in Jim & Nick's BBQ, a restaurant chain based in Birmingham, Alabama) and I came up with the idea to put together a team to compete at Memphis in May. Our mission: to take an entirely different path than most participants. We wanted to barbecue a whole hog using sustainably raised, better-tasting pork. We started with a Mangalista, the richly marbled Rolls-Royce of heirloom hog varieties. The meat wasn't injected with chemicals, aggressively seasoned, or drowned in a pool of cloying sauce. Instead it was minimally seasoned and cooked very slowly, to coax out the meat's richest flavor.

Dubbed the Fatback Collective, our eventual team boasted some serious talent, including Rodney Scott (Scott's Barbecue in Hemingway, South Carolina), Pat Martin (Martin's Bar-B-Que Joint in Nolensville, Tennessee), and Sam Jones (Skylight Inn in Ayden, North Carolina). These pitmasters are the real deal, and so is their barbecue. We also snagged writers John T. Edge and Wright Thompson, rancher Will Harris, and some of the best chefs in the South, including Sean Brock (Husk in Charleston, South Carolina), John Currence (City Grocery in Oxford, Mississippi), Ashley Christiansen (Poole's Diner, among others, in Raleigh, North Carolina), Drew Robinson (Jim & Nick's BBQ), Rob McDaniel (Spring House in Lake Martin, Alabama), and my business partners Steve Stryjewski and Ryan Prewitt. Together, we bonded over a shared goal to dial the competition back to what we perceived as the soul of Southern barbecue—not to mention a whole lot of bourbon. It was this same passion that led the Fatback Collective to Uruguay last year to cook with local chefs over open fires and natural wood. That trip had a big impact on me—I've learned more about barbecue and smoking in the last few years than I have in my entire life.

Cooking over fire is not about a recipe; it's much more intuitive than that. The whole hog we barbecued, for instance, took twenty-four hours—someone had to babysit that pig the entire time. You *really* get to know someone, and the animal that you're cooking, when you spend that many hours sitting around, talking shit, and drinking. As a result of these barbecue sessions, the members of our team have become my best friends for life, and I look forward to all of our future cookouts on the horizon.

The sauce issue is where the divide begins in the South. Texas is all about smoke and salt and beef brisket; sauce is an afterthought. Memphis sauce is sweet, and the Carolinas prefer a vinegar sauce. It all comes down to personal preference; everybody should eat what he or she likes. I like them all, depending on where I am and what I'm eating. It would be a boring world if all food tasted the same, so I embrace the differences.

One thing that almost everyone will agree on is temperature, time, and smoke. Low and slow is the only way to go. Cooking slowly allows meat to relax and become tender; cooking too hot and too fast will make it tough. Timing differs depending on the texture preference. Some like their ribs to still have some chew, whereas others like them falling off the bone. I've tasted fork-tender brisket that had cooked for eighteen hours, and the same cut at Kreuz's in Lockhart, Texas, where they cook at a slightly higher heat for six hours. I wouldn't pass up either.

This chapter includes some of my favorite preparations for family meals and backyard entertaining, from simple grilled chicken breasts (perked up with a lemony olive vinaigrette) to some crazy delicious sandwiches (trust me: they are totally worth the effort it takes to stoke a fire) to all-day smoking endeavors that lead to spectacular eating, like Beer-Smoked Beef Short Ribs (page 88). I cook all of these on my home grill, a round barrel setup with an offset sidecar box for burning wood and coals. This is a common grill in the South, but barbecue enthusiasts tend to have strong opinions and preferences about what type works best, from an inexpensive kettle grill to the bullet-shaped smokers popular on the competition circuits. As long as you pay attention to the temperature and the heat source, you'll have great results.

What follows is a quick grilling primer and a breakdown of the cooking methods that apply to all the recipes in this chapter.

LIGHTING CHARCOAL

The easiest way to light any kind of charcoal is with a chimney starter, an upright metal cylinder that protects and concentrates the heat. To use one, simply fill the space under the wire rack with some wadded-up paper and fill the rack above with charcoal. Light the paper and let the coals burn until they are lightly covered in white ash. Disperse them in the grill, according to your cooking method. Be sure to heat more coals (and wood chunks, see right) as needed, every 30 minutes or so.

COOKING METHODS

Quick and hot: When you want to grill small, tender pieces of meat that cook quickly, like steak, hamburgers, and chicken breasts, you need to prepare a grill for direct cooking, as these cuts do best when they're seared over hot coals. A good heat test is to hold your hand a few inches over the grill: For high heat (450°F to 550°F), you should be able to keep it there for 3 to 4 seconds before you need to move it; if you can leave your hand there for 5 to 6 seconds, then the grill is at medium heat (300°F to 400°F). The important thing to remember when cooking over high heat is to keep the meat high enough above the heat source to protect it from charring when the fire flares up.

Low and slow: For larger, tougher cuts of meat that require longer cooking times to become tender, such as roasts, whole birds, and ribs, you'll want to use moderate (225°F to 275°F), indirect heat that cooks in a much gentler way. Keep the coals in a small pile on one side of the grill (rather than spreading them out as you would when grilling steaks or hamburgers), opposite the top vent. (If the vent is in the center of the lid, put the coals in the front so it's easy to add to them.) Add wood chunks to the periphery of the coals so that they catch and burn slowly. Maintain a temperature between 250°F and 275°F for something that will cook for 4 to 6 hours, and 225°F for long smoking for brisket, short ribs, etc. Look for a gentle, steady ribbon of smoke coming from the grill.

For long smoking, a burn barrel or other offset fire is extremely helpful in creating a steady supply of hot coals to maintain smoking temperature.

ABOUT WOOD CHUNKS

Always use dry or "cured" wood; moist green wood will choke a fire with too much smoke. In the country I use old logs, when available, but for most backyard grilling I rely on wood chunks available at most hardware or grocery stores. Depending on how much smoky flavor you want and how long you'll be barbecuing, you'll want to add more chunks to the grill as they are depleted, every half hour or so.

Wood chips burn too quickly for slow cooking— reserve them for the smoke box of a gas grill.

Oak: The choice in central Texas, this native hardwood has a clean, even burn and a mild flavor that doesn't overpower the flavor of meat.

Hickory: It has a more pungent, smoky flavor than oak and a clean, even burn.

Mesquite: This wood has a pronounced, pungent flavor with a hot burn, so use it carefully to avoid fluctuating temperatures.

Fruit woods, such as apple and pecan: These can be overpowering for a long, slow cooking process. Use in moderation.

SMOKING ON A GAS GRILL

This is not my preferred method, but if it's your only option you can achieve good results using a smoke box and wood chips. Light the far right side of a gas grill, leaving the heating elements on the left side turned off (if your grill has three heating elements, shut the middle heat source off as well). Soak a bag of wood chips in water for about 30 minutes. Drain and put some in a smoker box. Put the smoker box over the heat source at the far right side of the grill. When the wood begins to smoke and the heat is between 225°F and 250°F, put the meat, fat-side up (if one side of the cut is thicker, as with brisket, position the thicker point closer to the heat), moving it to the left as much as possible. The meat should not be directly over the heat source.

Close the grill and do your best not to get anxious and peek (the thermometer gauge and a gentle, steady ribbon of smoke should let you know that the meat is smoking). Check the wood chips every 30 minutes or so, and replenish with a handful or two of soaked chips as needed (when the pile is more ash than glowing chips).

WHY BOTHER TO fire up the grill for a sandwich? How about if it's possibly the best sandwich in the world (with all due respect for our local muffalettas)?

Imagine crispy chicken with mayonnaise, a piquant olive spread, fresh lettuce, tomatoes, and a fried egg. The layers of flavor elevate this Uruguayan sandwich (traditionally made with pounded beef, but I prefer juicy chicken thighs) to something extraordinary.

CHICKEN CHIVITO SANDWICH
with Ham and Olive Spread

SERVES 4

4 (4-ounce) boneless, skin-on chicken thighs
About 5 tablespoons olive oil
Kosher salt and black pepper
4 rolls
4 large eggs
Olive Spread (recipe follows)
½ pound thinly sliced smoked ham
4 handfuls of arugula
4 slices of ripe tomato

Heat your grill to medium-high.

Lightly brush the chicken thighs with about 2 tablespoons of the oil and season with salt and pepper. Grill skin-side down until the skin is crispy and golden brown, about 6 minutes. Flip and grill until cooked through, about 2 minutes.

Slice the rolls in half and lightly brush the cut sides with about 1 tablespoon of the oil. Grill the halves oiled-side down until toasty and golden, a couple of minutes.

Meanwhile, fry the eggs. Heat the remaining 2 tablespoons oil in a medium skillet over medium heat. Add the eggs and fry to an over-medium consistency, about 1 minute on each side. Top each egg with a pinch each of salt and pepper.

Put the grilled chicken on the bottom halves of the rolls and spoon the olive spread on the top halves. Put ham slices on top of the chicken and then layer the fried eggs, arugula, and finally the tomato over the ham. Slap the top half over the chicken and you're ready to go.

Olive Spread

MAKES A GENEROUS ½ CUP

¼ cup pitted kalamata olives, quartered
¼ cup picholine olives, pitted and quartered
1 teaspoon sherry vinegar

Grated zest and juice of ½ lemon
½ teaspoon chopped fresh thyme
1 tablespoon mayonnaise
Pinch each of kosher salt and black pepper

Combine the ingredients in a bowl and refrigerate until needed (up to a day in advance).

THIS IS A Sunday house specialty of Ryan Prewitt, my former chef de cuisine, now partner in our restaurant group and chef at our newest restaurant, Pêche. He busted these out at an Herbsaint summer rosé party at his home. These chicken skewers are the perfect backyard dish; first, because they taste amazing, and second, because they're served on a stick so they're easy to eat. A "white" mayonnaise-based sauce is common in Alabama, and it's a delicious combination. The vinegar, pepper, and horseradish are surprising foils for the crispy, salty grilled chicken.

GRILLED CHICKEN
on a Stick with Alabama White Barbecue Sauce

MAKES 12 TO 16 SKEWERS

4 (about 6 ounces each) boneless, skin-on chicken thighs, pounded to ½-inch thickness

1 tablespoon vegetable oil

2 teaspoons kosher salt

½ teaspoon black pepper

Alabama White Barbecue Sauce (recipe follows)

Cut the thighs into even thirds or quarters, whatever makes sense for their individual shape. Brush the chicken with the oil, season with the salt and pepper, and weave the strips onto skewers.

Heat your grill to medium.

When the grill is hot, put the skewers on the grill skin-side down. Grill until the skin is nice and crispy, 8 to 10 minutes. Flip the thighs and finish cooking on the other side, an additional 3 to 5 minutes (the skewers should need 13 to 15 minutes total cooking time).

Brush the thighs with ¼ cup of the barbecue sauce and char on the grill for 30 seconds to 1 minute per side. Serve with a dish of the remaining sauce for dipping. Leftover sauce is delicious with any grilled meat (like pork chops, chicken breasts, or spare ribs).

Alabama White Barbecue Sauce

MAKES ABOUT 1½ CUPS

1 cup mayonnaise

½ cup white or cider vinegar

2 tablespoons cane syrup

1 tablespoon prepared
horseradish

1 teaspoon black pepper

1 teaspoon fresh lemon juice

½ teaspoon kosher salt

¼ teaspoon cayenne

½ jalapeño, stemmed, seeded,
and minced

1 tablespoon minced pickled
chiles

Combine the ingredients in
a bowl and whisk together.
Refrigerate for at least 1 hour
and up to 8 hours before
serving.

I AM AMAZED every time I eat chicken and olives at how perfectly the two ingredients pair together. This vinaigrette is a good alternative to barbecue sauce, and it makes for a nice, healthy meal without sacrificing satisfying flavor. The olives and vinegar provide a big punch, while still allowing the charred, juicy chicken meat to shine. I always serve this chicken with Fresh Mint Couscous (page 195).

GRILLED CHICKEN BREASTS
with Lemon-Olive Vinaigrette

SERVES 4

CHICKEN
4 (6- to 8-ounce) boneless, skin-on chicken breasts

3 tablespoons olive oil

1 teaspoon chopped fresh thyme

Grated zest of 1 lemon

1 teaspoon kosher salt

½ teaspoon black pepper

LEMON-OLIVE VINAIGRETTE
Grated zest and juice of 1 lemon

2 tablespoons sherry vinegar

¾ cup extra-virgin olive oil

½ cup pitted and chopped kalamata olives

¼ cup pitted and chopped green olives (such as picholine or lucques)

1 teaspoon chopped fresh thyme

Kosher salt and black pepper

Marinate the chicken: Combine the chicken breasts with the olive oil, thyme, lemon zest, salt, and pepper (you can do this in a zipper-top plastic bag or a covered baking dish) and marinate in the refrigerator for at least 1 hour and up to 4 hours.

Meanwhile, prepare the vinaigrette: Whisk together the lemon zest and juice, vinegar, olive oil, olives, thyme, and a generous pinch each of salt and pepper.

When you're ready to cook, heat your grill to medium.

Grill the breasts skin-side down until the skin is golden brown and pulls easily away from the grill, about 8 minutes. Use tongs to flip the breasts and grill the other side until cooked through (but not dry), an additional 4 to 5 minutes.

To serve, transfer the chicken breasts to a plate and top each with a couple spoonfuls of the vinaigrette.

RYAN AND I put these together on the fly while we were waiting a long eleven to twelve hours for the short ribs (page 88). Let's face it; if you're going to slow-smoke meat, and breathe in that delicious aroma the whole day, it's good to plan on some snacks to eat in the near term. These easy-to-assemble, succulent smoked thighs are just the thing, and they make for a very satisfying meal when paired with cold, dry pink or white wine, sliced tomatoes, a few pickled vegetables, and sharp cheese. You can also follow this method to smoke a whole chicken; it will need about 3½ hours.

SMOKED CHICKEN
Thighs

SERVES 4

2 pounds bone-in, skin-on chicken thighs

1 tablespoon plus 1 teaspoon kosher salt

1 teaspoon black pepper

½ teaspoon paprika

¼ teaspoon cayenne

Rinse the chicken and thoroughly blot dry with paper towels. Combine the salt, black pepper, paprika, and cayenne in a small bowl and season the chicken thighs with the spice mixture.

Set up your grill or smoker for low-and-slow cooking with wood chunks (see page 68).

Add the chicken, close the grill, and smoke at 225°F for about 2 hours, until the chicken is tender and pulls easily away from the bone. Add more hot coals and a few wood chunks every 30 minutes or so, and adjust the vents as needed to maintain a steady temperature.

RICH AND FULL of flavor, duck has always been one my favorite meats. I love it roasted, braised, and simmered in hearty hunter stews, and preserved as confit. This last method has become my new favorite—the smoke and slow cooking coax out and elevate the bird's deep flavors. I like to serve this smoked duck alongside rice (steamed or dirty) or roasted potatoes, or in killer sandwiches (I like mine slathered with a lemon-spiked mayo, topped with basil, pickled banana peppers, and arugula, on ciabatta). When it comes to smoking, I prefer aromatic hardwoods like hickory, oak, or pecan.

This recipe plays with the classic preparation of duck confit, or salting and slow-cooking ducks in their own fat. This method is for one duck, but if you're going to make the time investment to smoke, I'd suggest doing two birds, so you'll have one to eat immediately along with fantastic leftovers.

SMOKED DUCK
with Aromatic Salt

SERVES 4

1 (4½- to 5-pound) duck
1 tablespoon plus 1 teaspoon kosher salt
1 teaspoon black pepper
1 teaspoon ground allspice
1 teaspoon ground fennel seed
½ small onion, halved
1 satsuma or tangerine, halved

Set up your grill or smoker for low-and-slow cooking with wood chunks (see page 68).

Meanwhile, remove any organ meats from the duck, rinse it under cold water, and pat dry with paper towels. Combine the salt, pepper, allspice, and fennel and season the inside and outside of the duck with the mixture. Put the onion and satsuma pieces into the cavity.

Put the duck in the smoker, cover, and smoke until fully cooked (see Note), about 2 hours. Add more hot coals and a few wood chunks every 30 minutes or so, and adjust the vents as needed to maintain a steady temperature of 225°F.

Tent the duck with foil and allow to rest for at least 30 minutes before slicing. Remove the breast meat and slice thin. Remove the bones from the duck legs and slice the meat thin as well.

NOTE: To test duck for doneness, most people would use a meat thermometer. But I always go with the method that one of my mentors, Albert Tordjman, the former chef at Flying Saucer in San Francisco, taught me. Instead of relying on a thermometer, I insert a paring knife into the duck (between the leg and the thigh) and then touch the knife to my lips or forearm to gauge the pure heat it throws off. For medium to medium-rare (125°F to 130°F), the knife should be warm but not uncomfortably hot. For duck, however, the desired temp of 155°F to 160°F will burn your lips, so test the knife against your forearm.

IT'S A GOOD thing quail tastes so good because it sure is a little bitty bird. I tend to think of quail as finger food—really delicious finger food. Grilling quail brings out its rich, dark-meat flavor in a big way. The key to good grilled quail is to rely on a hot, quick fire but keep the birds far enough from the flames so they don't burn.

The addition of arugula and grilled peaches creates a beautiful combination that can serve as an appetizer or a meal. But to be honest, I tend to grill quail so my friends and I have something to snack on while we're cooking a main course that takes a bit more time. They're like some fancy form of chicken wings, to be ripped apart and eaten with our hands.

SPICY GRILLED QUAIL
with Grilled Peaches

SERVES 6 AS AN APPETIZER OR 3 AS A MAIN DISH

6 semi-boneless quail
Kosher salt and black pepper
2 tablespoons balsamic vinegar
1 tablespoon honey
1 tablespoon plus 1 teaspoon olive oil
1 teaspoon chopped fresh rosemary
1 teaspoon chopped fresh thyme
1 teaspoon red pepper flakes
3 ripe peaches, halved and pitted
4 generous handfuls of arugula

Rinse the quail and pat dry with paper towels. Clip the wing joint off each quail if desired. (If you leave the wing on, it can get in the way of charring the skin, and you can't eat it anyway; once cooked it's like a toothpick). Season the quail with salt and pepper.

In a small bowl, whisk together the balsamic vinegar, honey, 1 tablespoon of the olive oil, the rosemary, thyme, and red pepper flakes. Transfer the mixture to a large zipper-top bag and add the quail. Refrigerate for 2 to 3 hours (or up to 8 hours) to allow the flavors to infuse the meat.

Heat your grill to high.

Remove the quail from the marinade. Pour the marinade into a saucepan, bring to a boil, and cook for 1 minute; set aside to cool.

Grill the quail until the meat starts to feel firm and the skin has a nice dark brown color, 2 to 3 minutes per side. The goal is to cook the meat to medium.

Brush the peach halves with the remaining 1 teaspoon olive oil and grill cut-side down until charred and slightly caramelized, 3 to 5 minutes.

Serve the quail on a bed of arugula with the grilled peach halves and a drizzle of the cooked marinade.

SOME OF YOU might be confused about this one. A grilled pork sandwich, seasoned with a commercial spice blend and served on white sandwich bread with mayo? Even I am confused about it. On paper, it doesn't make sense, but I can count on my hands how many meals excite me as much as this sandwich. I think of it as one of the Great Wonders of the World.

I first had this combination in north Baton Rouge at a small grocery after playing basketball with some friends. Holy shit. I didn't see it again until years later, when my coozan (code for Cajun cousin) Billy Link and I were in Mamou on Mardi Gras day, and we caught the intoxicating aroma of grilled meats in the air. He stuck his nose in the air and said, "Man, I hope that's a pork steak sandwich." It was.

We tracked the smell to a small group of people grilling in a roll-up-door garage, and there it was. We asked whom they were cooking for, hoping for an invite, and it turned out they were cooking for anyone who happened to be walking by. Score! I jumped on the grill and started making sandwiches for everyone and remembered how amazing this simple combination could be, especially standing in a garage on a rainy day in Mamou with new friends.

MAMOU GRILLED PORK STEAK
Sandwich

SERVES 4

4 pork shoulder steaks, each 4 to 5 ounces and about 1 inch thick

2 teaspoons Tony Chachere's Original Creole Seasoning, or other Cajun spice blend

Soft white bread

Mayonnaise

About 30 minutes before cooking, pull the pork steaks from the fridge and season them generously with the spice blend.

Heat your grill to medium-high.

Sear the steaks on each side over the hottest part of the grill (you want a nice char on the meat), 4 to 5 minutes per side, and then move them to a cooler area to finish cooking through more slowly, 6 to 8 minutes more.

Serve the pork steaks between slices of soft white bread and don't be shy with the mayo.

TENDERLOINS ARE NICE and tender, but whether pork or deer, they tend to be lacking in the flavor department. Marinating the tenderloins helps impart character to an otherwise lackluster piece of meat. The lemony dressing and spicy bite of the arugula make this dish pop. This is a good meal for family-style cookouts because it's easy (and pretty) to serve on a platter and let everyone dig in.

GRILLED PORK TENDERLOINS
with Arugula and Parmesan

SERVES 4

PORK

2 (8-ounce) pork tenderloins

3 tablespoons olive oil

2 tablespoons Worcestershire sauce

2 tablespoons apple cider vinegar

1 tablespoon honey

2 tablespoons sugar

2 garlic cloves, thinly sliced

2 teaspoons dried oregano

2 teaspoons kosher salt

2 teaspoons black pepper

1 teaspoon paprika

ARUGULA SALAD

2 tablespoons extra-virgin olive oil

Juice of 1 lemon

Pinch each of kosher salt and black pepper

8 cups loosely packed arugula

¼ cup shaved Parmesan slices

Marinate the pork: Combine the tenderloins and all of the marinade ingredients in a large zipper-top plastic bag, and work with your hands to completely coat the meat. Marinate in the refrigerator for at least 2 hours (and up to 8 hours), massaging the mixture every hour or so to distribute the liquid.

Heat your grill to high.

Grill the tenderloins, using tongs to roll the meat every 2 minutes to allow it to char evenly, until cooked to medium, about 15 minutes total. Transfer to a plate, tent with foil, and allow the meat to rest for 5 to 7 minutes.

Make the arugula salad: While the meat is resting, whisk together the extra-virgin olive oil, lemon juice, and salt and pepper in a large salad bowl. Add the arugula and toss well to combine.

To serve, thinly slice the pork and arrange it on a serving platter. Top the meat with arugula salad and the shaved Parmesan.

FROM SWEET AND sour pork in neighborhood Chinese restaurants to pineapple-glazed ham in spring, pork's affinity for fruit (perked up with a bit of acid) is well established. For good reason—the fatty nature of good pork (ideally heirloom breeds, not the lean, flavorless "other white meat") loves vinegar and sugar. In this recipe, I like how the light sweetness of Steen's Louisiana Cane Vinegar (it's oak-aged and has a mellow flavor) echoes the sweetness of the dried fruit, but you can also use sherry wine vinegar. Traditionally hogs were butchered in the late fall, when there's not a lot of fruit left on the trees, so I use dried figs, raisins, and apricots in this recipe with great results. The interplay of aromatic spices, vinegar, mustard, and fresh citrus creates a delicious sauce for the grilled meat.

GRILLED PORK CHOPS
with Sweet and Sour Dried Fruit

SERVES 4

4 (12-ounce) bone-in pork chops with the fat cap

Kosher salt and black pepper

12 dried black Mission figs, stems trimmed

½ cup raisins

½ cup dried apricots

1 lemon wedge plus 1 teaspoon fresh lemon juice

1 cup cane or sherry wine vinegar

2 tablespoons light brown sugar

2 teaspoons coriander seeds, toasted and coarsely cracked

½ teaspoon cayenne

1 (3-inch) rosemary sprig

1 tablespoon whole-grain mustard

1 teaspoon balsamic vinegar

Generously season the chops with salt and black pepper; set aside.

Combine the figs, raisins, and apricots with the lemon wedge, cane vinegar, sugar, coriander, cayenne, and 1 cup water in a small saucepan. Bring the mixture to a boil over medium heat, then reduce the heat to low, and simmer until the fruit is soft, about 20 minutes. Strain the fruit (reserving the liquid separately) and cool.

Return the vinegar mixture to the pan, add the rosemary sprig, and bring to a simmer over medium-low heat. Cook until reduced to about ¼ cup, about 6 minutes. Stir the mustard, balsamic vinegar, and lemon juice into the reduction. Quarter the figs and slice the apricots into thirds. Add the fruit to the vinegar mixture, remove the rosemary sprig, and set the fruit aside at room temperature (do not refrigerate).

Heat your grill to high.

Grill the chops on both sides until well charred and just cooked through to medium, 9 to 10 minutes total. You'll want to leave the chops in one place long enough to mark the exterior, but be prepared to move them with tongs if the rendered fat starts a flare-up.

Transfer the chops to a platter, cover with foil, and let rest for at least 5 minutes. Serve each chop with a few spoonfuls of the dried fruit mixture and sauce.

WHENEVER I'M BACK home in Southwest Louisiana, I'm always amazed at the cuts of meat available in the grocery stores there that I can't find in urban markets in New Orleans: pigs feet, pork necks, whole bone-in hams, and huge bone-in ham steaks.

A ham steak may be one of the most underutilized and underappreciated options for the grill—or dinner, for that matter. It's extremely cheap, super delicious, and quick—it takes about 10 minutes to cook. When buying a ham steak, look for one with the bone in the middle (that may be the only way you can find it). Or have the butcher slice a bone-in ham ½ to ¾ inch thick.

I really like the addition of the charred oranges here, but Sweet and Sour Spring Onions (page 193) are another great option.

GRILLED HAM STEAK
with Charred Blood Oranges

SERVES 1 OR 2

1 pound ham steak (½ to ¾ inch thick)

1 teaspoon vegetable oil

1½ teaspoons barbecue rub, such as Texas Campfire Dry Rub (page 85), or your favorite brand

2 teaspoons sugar

1 large blood orange or navel orange

Heat your grill to medium.

Evenly coat the ham steak with the oil and seasoning rub. Sear the steak until it's well charred, about 5 minutes on each side.

Meanwhile, put the sugar out on a small plate, slice the orange in half, and dip each half, cut-side down, into the sugar to coat. Grill the orange halves alongside the ham, cut-side down, until they char and begin to caramelize, 5 to 10 minutes.

Transfer the ham steak to a platter and rub it with the charred orange halves while squeezing out the juice from each half.

I LOVE ROASTED lamb sirloin, lamb chops, and grilled lamb steaks, but grilled lamb saddle trumps them all. This is the meal to prepare when you really want to impress dinner guests with a dish that's a bit more involved and unexpected. You should be able to find lamb saddle at a good meat market or from your favorite lamb producer at the farmer's market.

What makes this dish so luxurious and delicious is the fact that you're wrapping the fatty belly around the tenderloin and the loin, the most tender parts of the lamb. The smoke and the slow cooking give you results that you could not get in any conventional oven. This dish is especially delicious served with Cajun Macaroni Salad (page 199) or Fresh Mint Couscous (page 195).

GRILLED BONELESS LAMB
Saddle

SERVES 4 TO 6

1 (5- to 7-pound) boneless lamb saddle with belly attached

6 garlic cloves

Grated zest of 1 lemon

Kosher salt and black pepper

3 anchovy fillets

1 teaspoon chopped fresh rosemary

Trim the excess fat from inside the saddle and from the bellies. Split the whole saddle lengthwise down the middle to form two long equal sections.

Combine the garlic, lemon zest, 1 teaspoon salt, the anchovies, and rosemary in a mortar and mash to a paste with a pestle. Season the inside of each saddle section with half of the paste, 1 teaspoon salt, and ½ teaspoon pepper.

Roll up each half, roulade-style, and tie with kitchen string. Each half will have a piece of loin and tenderloin, with the belly surrounding it. Season the outsides with 1 teaspoon salt and ½ teaspoon pepper.

Heat your grill to high.

Slowly and evenly sear the roulade over the hot side, turning as needed, until deeply and evenly browned. Move the lamb to the cooler side of the grill (about 225°F), cover, and grill, rotating periodically to ensure even cooking, until cooked through to medium (145°F), about 2 hours. Add more hot coals as needed, every 30 minutes or so. The total time will vary based on the heat of the grill; if you need to lower the temperature, lift the cover.

Transfer the meat to a cutting board and tent with foil; let rest for at least 10 minutes. Cut the lamb into ½-inch slices and serve.

THERE ARE SEVERAL varieties of ovens, spits, and grills that you can use to cook a leg of lamb. Most people use a conventional oven because it's easiest, so this recipe is tailored to that option. But I love to cook this leg of lamb on my grill, which has a sidecar smoker; the grill takes a bit longer than the oven (four hours instead of about one and a half) but delivers extraordinary flavors. The basic cooking concept applies to any method: Begin with a very high heat and then reduce to a low-and-slow heat to finish cooking. The goal in cooking slowly is for the leg of lamb to be rosy pink all the way through, a perfect medium (145°F), which is what I prefer for lamb (as opposed to medium-rare).

The flavors and inspiration for this recipe came from a visit to a lamb rancher outside of Austin. Consider serving the meat Texas-style, with pinto beans, coleslaw, warm tortillas, and red salsa on the side.

ROAST LEG OF LAMB
with Texas Campfire Dry Rub

SERVES 6 TO 8

1 (7- to 10-pound) bone-in leg of lamb

3 tablespoons olive oil

½ cup Texas Campfire Dry Rub (recipe follows)

An hour before cooking, remove the lamb from the refrigerator, massage the entire leg with the olive oil and the dry rub, and let stand at room temperature.

Heat the oven to 450°F.

Put the leg of lamb on a rack on a roasting pan or rimmed baking sheet and roast for 15 minutes.

Remove the leg from the oven and reduce the temperature to 300°F. Once the oven temp is down, put the lamb back in the oven and cook until medium, an internal temperature of 145°F, 1 to 1½ hours.

To allow the juices to settle back into the meat, tent the meat with foil and let it rest for about 30 minutes before slicing.

Texas Campfire Dry Rub

MAKES ABOUT 1½ CUPS

This warmly spiced rub is delicious with lamb, venison, and beef (consider using it on a chuck roast).

½ cup kosher salt
3 tablespoons black pepper
2 tablespoons ground fennel seed
1 tablespoon ground cumin
1 teaspoon ground cinnamon
3 tablespoons chili powder
2 tablespoons dried oregano
1 tablespoon sugar

Combine all ingredients. Store in a tightly sealed container for up to 3 months.

I've eaten some great lamb in my life. In fact, I can think of several instances when I thought, "Okay this is it—the best lamb ever!" My most recent episode of lamb nirvana was on a ranch just west of Austin, Texas. A rancher who had about sixty head of dorper lamb, a hearty breed that thrives in arid climates, produced the meat and also a llama named Fritz (llamas are commonly thrown in with goats or sheep to provide the herd with leadership and protection). I liked Fritz—I haven't met a whole lot of llamas, but of the ones I've seen up close, he's the only one that didn't try to eat my shirt.

The most memorable detail about the lamb, however, is how flavorful it was. When you buy a lamb or any animal from the source, from the farmer who raised it, you tend to *really* pay attention to how you cook it and use every inch of that animal with the highest degree of respect.

After a full day of learning about the peculiarities of this particular breed and the challenges of raising them in the Texas Hill Country, we took a full carcass with us to nearby Montesino Ranch, a small organic farm in Wimberley, Texas, for an old-fashioned Texas cookout, complete with a beautiful wood-fired sidecar grill, outdoor kitchen, good bourbon, and really great company. As if this wasn't enough to set the scene for a beautiful night, we closed the evening gathered around a crackling campfire

LAMB UNDER THE LIVE OAKS ON A TEXAS RANCH

with two guitar-strumming musicians singing and playing late into the night. It was like we were living inside the Eagles song "Seven Bridges Road"—but that might be the bourbon talking.

A lot of people ask me where I get my ideas from, and what inspires me. Well, this particular night pretty much sums it up. Driving to Wimberley, I had no idea how I was going to prepare the lamb, or what I was going to serve with it, nor did I want to until I saw what was in season in their garden and the cooking setup available to me. I always prefer to let the ingredients tell me what to do. Montesino specializes in some really amazing organic produce—when I was there the fields were bursting with sweet cabbage, carrots, peppery arugula, herbs, and radishes. Working with a whole lamb and great produce provides lots of opportunities to try new dishes and prepare different parts of the animal in different ways. The most memorable flavors from that meal were from this slow-cooked leg of lamb.

Before we stumbled off to bed that night I stoked the fire on the pit to cook the other parts of the lamb that take a good while, including the neck, the ribs, and so forth. The next morning we had tender, smoky lamb carnitas breakfast tacos (made with fresh, rich duck eggs) with some killer cilantro salsa verde from the farmers at Montesino.

WHEN IT COMES to cooking short ribs outside, the basic idea is to infuse the meat with smoke and then put the ribs in a high-sided, covered pan to slow-cook the rest of the way. As with all fatty meats, slow is good for coaxing out flavor and making the ribs tender. The cooking time may vary here. To test for doneness, gently pinch the meat on the sides to see if it gives; that's when it's done. If the meat still feels hard, that's because it is—give it a little longer.

These short ribs are an all-day event—they cook for about eleven hours—and you'll need something to snack on when you're hanging by the grill. Try the Smoked Chicken Thighs on page 73. (On that note, you'll also want to choose your company wisely, as they'll be hanging out for the entire day, too. . . .)

BEER-SMOKED
Beef Short Ribs

SERVES 6 TO 8

3 tablespoons kosher salt

1½ tablespoons sugar

1 tablespoon black pepper

2 teaspoons cayenne

8 to 10 pounds beef short ribs, cut along the bone, 1 to 1½ pounds each

2 onions

1 carrot

3 (6-inch) rosemary branches

2 (12-ounce) bottles of beer (lager or dark, as you prefer)

Combine the salt, sugar, black pepper, and cayenne in a large mixing bowl. Add the ribs and toss until the pieces are somewhat evenly coated. Set aside to marinate while you light the fire.

Set up your grill or smoker for low-and-slow cooking with wood chunks (see page 68).

When the wood begins to smolder, put the ribs directly over the heat, close the grill, and smoke at 225°F for 3 hours. Add more hot coals and a few wood chunks every 30 minutes or so, and adjust the vents as needed to maintain a steady temperature.

Dice the onions and carrot and put them in a large aluminum pan with the rosemary and beer.

Transfer the ribs to the aluminum pan, cover the pan with foil, and return to the grill. Smoke for about 8 more hours (adding more hot coals and a few wood chunks every 30 minutes or so, and adjusting the vents as needed to maintain a steady temperature of 250°F to 275°F), until the meat is very tender and pulls away easily from the bone.

Serve the ribs with a few spoonfuls of the rich braising liquid.

ROAST, BRAISE, SIMMER, and FRY

BRAISED CHICKEN WITH SALAMI AND OLIVES 95

Guinea Hen Gumbo 96

SMOTHERED CHICKEN 97

Hunter's Style Braised Duck 98

SLOW-ROASTED PORK SHOULDER WITH KUMQUATS AND CHILES 100

Lamb Shoulder Stew with Lemons and Olives 102

TUPELO HONEY–GLAZED HAM 103

Crispy Pork Cutlets with Brown Butter, Lemon, and Sage 105

PORK BELLY AND SMOKED SAUSAGE CASSOULET 106

Braised and Crispy Goat with Yogurt Sauce, Cucumbers, and Mint 108

When we visited family and friends when I was a kid, I was always impressed by how much food everyone had prepared. These days, if we go to someone's house for dinner, it usually consists of something pretty straightforward, a one-dish type of deal, unless it's Aunt Sally's house. She always does it old school, with some sort of main-dish meat, roasted or braised, at least two side dishes, homemade rolls, and two desserts. And there's extra of everything—just in case more people show up and everyone wants seconds. Even so there are still leftovers, which get packed up and sent home with guests.

Most of the recipes in this chapter are designed with Aunt Sally's style—which also happens to be mine—in mind. Southerners have always been fans of the fatty and tougher meats, because they're the cuts with the most character and flavor. My grandparents had lots of kids, and other family members to feed, so they weren't going to Whole Foods to buy sustainably fished salmon. They were buying big pieces of pork and beef shoulders that could feed plenty of people out of one pot. They learned how to coax out flavor through slow cooking, and served the meats with rich, delicious gravies to be sopped up with rolls, cornbread, or rice.

The other major bonus of these recipes is that the prep takes place well before the meal is served, before any one shows up, so you're free when they do arrive. And you look like a pro when you pull something delectable out of the oven or off the stove, all ready to go, and say, "It was nothing."

These slow-simmered preparations embody the soul of Southern cooking. For me, the kitchen is the heart of a house and any get-together or family time—that's what makes a home-cooked meal so special. Some of the best times of my life have revolved around a kitchen table, watching my mom or grandad cook, and later cooking with my own children. The kitchen is where everyone can relax and have fun. At any get-together at my house, you'll find me in front of the stove, because that's where the action is. I guess that's why I chose chef as my profession.

YOU MAY BE wondering what this recipe has to do with Southern food. Good question. New Orleans has a sizable Sicilian population, and if you're ever around the suburbs of New Orleans, you'll notice that the accents sound more like Brooklyn than South Louisiana. The "burbs" is also where you'll also find numerous "red sauce" Italian restaurants. My wife's grandmother's chicken cacciatore was one of her signature dishes. I like this dish because it's a great use of local chicken and the amazing and awesome salami that Cochon Butcher makes. I'm also a salt fanatic and really like the way the olives and salami add layers of salty flavor that you cannot get from the seasoning alone.

BRAISED CHICKEN
with Salami and Olives

SERVES 4 TO 6

1 (3½- to 4-pound) chicken,
  cut into 10 pieces
2½ teaspoons kosher salt
¾ teaspoon black pepper
2 tablespoons olive oil
1 medium onion, sliced
5 garlic cloves, thinly sliced
½ fennel bulb, thinly sliced
1 (8-inch) rosemary branch
1¼ cups diced salami
1 cup green olives, cut in half
1 teaspoon dried oregano
½ teaspoon red pepper flakes
½ cup dry white wine
2 tablespoons tomato paste
2 tablespoons all-purpose flour
2¼ cups chicken broth
4 bay leaves
Juice of 1 lemon

Heat the oven to 375°F.

Season the chicken with the salt and pepper. Heat the olive oil in a large skillet over medium heat and sear the chicken in 2 batches until golden brown, about 7 minutes per side. Transfer the cooked chicken to a 9 × 13-inch baking dish.

Add the onion to the skillet and cook in the rendered chicken fat, stirring, until brown, about 4 minutes. Add the garlic, fennel, rosemary, salami, olives, oregano, and red pepper flakes. Pour in the wine and simmer to reduce, scraping the bottom of the pan. Add the tomato paste and cook for 5 minutes. Add the flour and cook, stirring to incorporate, for another 2 minutes.

Pour in the chicken broth in batches and stir to incorporate. Bring to a simmer over medium heat and cook until slightly thickened, 2 to 3 minutes. Stir in the bay leaves and lemon juice.

Pour the sauce over the chicken in the baking dish and roast in the oven, basting every 30 minutes, until the chicken is very tender, about 1½ hours. Discard the bay leaves.

Serve the chicken warm, with plenty of the sauce.

THE WORLD KNOWS that New Orleans is the epicenter for flying beads and the colorful, boozy spectacle that is Mardi Gras. But if you want to escape the crowds, drive a couple hours west, and you'll discover an entirely different version of the same holiday: the Courir de Mardi Gras, which translates as "the run of Fat Tuesday," in which masked, costumed men on horseback ride from farm to farm, asking for ingredients to make gumbo.

These days, when there is no real need to forage for ingredients, the tradition is more symbolic, and involves lots of zydeco music, cold beer, and chicken chasing.

The Courir de Mardi Gras takes place every year, and it's a deep part of the culture here. Although the chickens they catch don't end up in the gumbo pot anymore (they're released and probably have a lot to work out in therapy), there is still a huge batch of community gumbo being simmered to share after the run. This gumbo recipe is different from what I usually make in that it is lighter and brothier, and more like the traditional country, Cajun-style gumbo. In Cajun country, guinea hens always come from someone's farm; they're never commercially produced, so the meat has an exceptional flavor and character.

GUINEA HEN
Gumbo

SERVES 8 TO 10

2½ cups vegetable oil

3½ cups all-purpose flour

2 whole guinea hens

½ pound bacon, diced

4 cups diced onions

2 cups diced celery

2 cups diced, seeded poblano chiles

¼ cup kosher salt

2 tablespoons black pepper

2 teaspoons cayenne

1½ pounds andouille sausage, halved lengthwise and sliced into ½-inch half moons

2 tablespoons hot sauce

Make the roux: Heat a 3-gallon heavy-bottomed pot over medium heat. Warm the oil and then whisk in the flour. Reduce the heat to medium-low and stir continuously until the roux is a deep, dirty-penny brown, without a trace of black, 1 to 1¼ hours.

Meanwhile, cut each guinea hen into 14 pieces: First, remove the outer wings at the joint and then remove the drumstick portion of the wing that is attached to the breast. Remove the whole legs and separate the drumsticks from the thighs. Using your knife, crack through the ribs from front to back; remove the breast plate. Cut the breast plate in half, and then cut each piece in half. Finally, remove the thighbone portion from the ribs. Discard the ribs.

When the roux is the right color, add the bacon, onions, celery, poblanos, salt, black pepper, and cayenne and cook, stirring, for about 5 minutes. Slowly whisk in 2 gallons water, making sure to fully incorporate the roux. Bring to a simmer, skimming any fat as the gumbo heats up. Add the guinea hens and the andouille, and return the gumbo to a slow simmer. Continuously skim any fat that rises to the surface. The hens and sausage will release quite a bit of fat. Cook until the guinea hen is completely tender, about 2 hours.

Add the hot sauce. The gumbo is now ready to serve, but it is much better if it is cooled and reheated the next day.

THIS DISH IS Southern home cooking at its best—simple, inexpensive ingredients transformed into a deeply satisfying meal. I think of this recipe as a confluence of the Southern and Cajun cooking styles that shaped my childhood. The slow-simmered melding of humble foods suggests the South Alabama country cooking that my grandad favored, but the rich gravy is thickened with a roux, as my granny from Louisiana would have done. Served over hot steamed rice, this is an ideal weeknight supper—my kids love to eat it as much as I do.

I find it fascinating that this Southern country dish is so similar to a chicken fricassee from France. Throw in a few potatoes, pearl onions, and carrots, serve it in a pretty Le Creuset crock, and it becomes a classic bistro dish.

SMOTHERED
Chicken

SERVES 4 TO 6

Kosher salt and black pepper
¼ teaspoon cayenne
1 (3½- to 4-pound) chicken, cut into 8 pieces (bone-in)
¼ cup vegetable oil
¼ cup all-purpose flour
1 medium onion, sliced
1 jalapeño, stemmed, seeded, and diced small
2 garlic cloves, minced
2 bay leaves
1 teaspoon dried thyme
2 teaspoons hot sauce
1 quart chicken broth
Steamed rice

Combine 1½ teaspoons salt, ½ teaspoon black pepper, and the cayenne in a small bowl; sprinkle the seasonings over the chicken pieces.

Heat the oil in a Dutch oven (preferably cast iron) over medium-high heat. Dredge the chicken in the flour, shaking off the excess. Save the leftover flour. When the oil is hot and slightly smoking, fry the chicken pieces in batches (so you don't crowd the pan), until golden, about 5 minutes. Use tongs to transfer the chicken to a plate lined with paper towels.

Once all of the chicken has been fried, add the remaining flour to the oil in the pot and cook, stirring, over medium-low heat to create a medium-brown roux, 4 to 5 minutes. Add the onion, jalapeño, garlic, bay leaves, thyme, and hot sauce, and cook for 3 minutes more. Pour in the broth and bring to a simmer while stirring carefully. Return the chicken to the pot and simmer, covered, very slowly until the chicken is fork tender, 1 to 1½ hours.

Taste the sauce and add more salt or pepper as desired. Serve the chicken over hot steamed rice, topped with plenty of the sauce.

THROUGHOUT THE SOUTH, hunting clubs are where men get together to be men. There are guns, whiskey, beer, football, naps, beer, hunting, beer, and lots of bullshit. If you're not already friends with someone you meet at a hunting club, then you will be when you leave.

Other than the entertaining company on hunting trips, the best part has got to be the eating. You'd be surprised how many amazing, camouflage-clad cooks there are in a duck camp. These men probably couldn't bake you a cake, but they can sure as hell cook up some game.

This recipe adheres to all the important elements of a hunting camp recipe. First, it should be based around something that you've hunted; second, it gets panfried; and third, it's thickened with a roux. After that, it's dealer's choice on additional meat, bacon, sausage, vegetables, and spices. When you don't want the final dish to taste too gamy, smoked meats and spice help balance the wild flavors.

This rustic preparation uses the entire duck, and benefits from the addition of the livers and backbone. You may need to adjust the amount of chicken broth, depending on how tightly the pot lid fits, as you want to end up with a rich, slightly thickened gravy to serve with the duck. This dish is great over steamed rice or fresh pappardelle.

I've called for farmed duck in this recipe, to make it easier for nonhunters to make at home—or out of season. Wild ducks tend be a bit smaller, so you may need a couple.

HUNTER'S STYLE
Braised Duck

SERVES 4

1 (4- to 5-pound) duck
2½ tablespoons kosher salt
1 tablespoon plus 1 teaspoon black
   pepper
¾ teaspoon cayenne
2 tablespoons vegetable oil
1 cup diced bacon
1 large onion, cut into large dice
6 cups quartered cremini
   mushrooms
1 tablespoon chopped fresh thyme
5 garlic cloves, sliced
3 tablespoons tomato paste
½ cup dry sherry

2 tablespoons brandy
¼ cup all-purpose flour
3 cups chicken broth
¼ cup red wine vinegar
6 bay leaves
1 tablespoon dried oregano

Rinse the duck under cold water and pat dry with paper towels. Remove the neck and liver and set aside. Put the duck breast-side down on a cutting board. Using poultry shears, remove the backbone by cutting on both sides of the bone. Alternatively, you can stand the duck upright and use a heavy knife to cut out the spine. Reserve the backbone.

Using a chef's knife, remove the ribs, leaving the breast plate intact.

Cut the duck into 8 pieces by first splitting the bird in half. Remove the whole wings and then cut each breast in half. Finally, separate the drumstick from the thigh.

Mix together the salt, black pepper, and cayenne. Season the duck pieces with half of the spice mixture.

To cook the duck, heat the oil in a large pot, preferably cast iron, over medium-high heat. Working in small batches, sear the duck, including the neck, backbone, and liver, over medium-high heat until well browned, 5 to 8 minutes. Use tongs to transfer the cooked pieces to a plate lined with paper towels.

Pour off and discard the oil from the pan, making sure that the crusty browned bits remain. Add the bacon and cook until rendered, 3 to 5 minutes.

Add the onion and mushrooms, season with the remaining spice mixture, and cook, stirring, until the onion is soft and the mushrooms have started to color, 5 to 7 minutes. Add the thyme and garlic and cook for a few minutes to soften. Add the tomato paste and cook, stirring, for a few minutes to incorporate.

Pour in the sherry and brandy, reduce the heat to medium-low, and simmer until the liquid is reduced, 3 to 4 minutes. Sprinkle the flour into the pot and stir to combine. Cook, stirring, for a few minutes to fully incorporate the flour. Add the chicken broth in small batches, stirring well.

Add the meat, bones, vinegar, bay leaves, and oregano. Bring to a simmer, then turn the heat to low, cover, and cook until the duck is fully tender, 2½ to 3 hours. Serve the meat with plenty of the rich gravy.

ONE OF THE benefits of farming at the mouth of the Mississippi is the topsoil that is deposited along the banks of the river between New Orleans and the Gulf of Mexico. This rich soil makes for what I consider to be some of the best citrus the world has to offer. Driving south from here there are miles of large, lush citrus groves producing oranges, blood oranges, satsumas, grapefruit, and kumquats. My favorite farmer in this region is Isabelle Cossart. She has ruined me for other citrus. Of all the great fruit in this region, she seems to have something special going on her grove. The kumquats impart a unique citrus flavor in this recipe, which is a great way to lighten up the flavor of what is usually a heavy dish.

SLOW-ROASTED PORK SHOULDER
with Kumquats and Chiles

SERVES 8

1 (6-pound) boneless pork shoulder
¼ cup kosher salt
1 tablespoon ground coriander
1 tablespoon paprika
1 tablespoon sugar
1 cup thinly sliced kumquats
10 garlic cloves, thinly sliced
4 jalapeños, thinly sliced into rounds
2 onions, sliced into ½-inch rounds

Heat the oven to 300°F. Using a chef's knife, make a series of 1-inch incisions on both sides of the shoulder (there should be about 15 per side).

Combine the salt, coriander, paprika, and sugar in a small bowl and use it to evenly season the pork, making sure to include the inside cavity where the bone was. Work the kumquats, garlic, and jalapeños into the center cavity and the incisions, massaging in the seasonings as you go.

Evenly cover the bottom of a large shallow roasting pan with the sliced onions. Put the shoulder on the onions and transfer to the oven. Roast, basting the pork with the fat and juices that collect in the pan, until the meat is very tender and caramelized, about 1½ hours.

Reduce the oven temperature to 275°F, add 4 cups water to the pan, and cover the pork with foil. Bake for 7 more hours, until the pork is fork tender.

Remove the pork from the pan and pour all the pan juices and scrapings into a saucepan. Skim the fat from the top and simmer over medium heat to reduce the liquid by half.

Serve the pork on a platter (it will be very tender and will likely pull apart into pieces) with the reduced sauce poured over the top.

CERTAIN TYPES OF meat are tied to ancient pairings that are so perfect, you understand their centuries of popularity. One is lamb, olives, and tomatoes. The brine of the olives, brightened by acid from the tomatoes, is a perfect counterpoint to the rich meat. The result is a luscious stew that's all about balance and layers of flavors.

You can simmer this stew on the stove, in the oven, or over a low fire on the grill. The only requirement is that you cook it slowly, simmering the meat until it becomes buttery and fork tender. Serve this over creamy grits or polenta with a good red wine.

LAMB SHOULDER STEW

with Lemons and Olives

SERVES 6 TO 8

6 pounds lamb shoulder

3 tablespoons kosher salt

2 teaspoons black pepper

1 teaspoon cayenne

1 teaspoon ground fennel seed

¼ cup olive oil

1 large onion, diced

6 plum tomatoes, diced

5 garlic cloves, thinly sliced

2 teaspoons finely chopped
    fresh rosemary

Grated zest of 2 lemons

6 anchovy fillets, minced

2 cups pitted black olives
    (such as kalamata)

1 cup dry white wine

⅓ cup all-purpose flour

1 quart chicken broth

Use a sharp knife to trim the sinew from the shoulder and then cut the meat into 3-inch cubes. Put the lamb in a large mixing bowl. Combine the salt, black pepper, cayenne, and fennel in a small bowl and then sprinkle the seasonings over the lamb. Toss until evenly coated.

Heat the olive oil in a large Dutch oven over medium-high heat. When the oil is hot and shimmering, sear the lamb in batches, so as not to crowd the pan, until nicely browned, 3 to 5 minutes per side. Transfer the meat to a plate lined with paper towels.

Pour out all but 3 tablespoons of fat from the pot. Add the onion, tomatoes, garlic, rosemary, lemon zest, anchovies, olives, and wine. Bring the mixture to a gentle simmer and cook until the wine is reduced by two-thirds, about 4 minutes.

Add the flour and stir until the mixture is evenly coated. Add the lamb and chicken broth and bring the mixture to a boil. Reduce the heat to low, cover, and simmer for about 2 hours.

Remove the cover (to allow the sauce to reduce) and cook until the meat is completely tender, an additional 2 hours.

WHEN I WAS young I had a terrible encounter with a bunch of wasps in a field out in the country. So when I tell you that I once held a tray of honeybees, without a bee suit, trust me, it took *a lot* for me to do this. This went down at Donald Smiley Apiary in Wewahitchka, Florida, where I learned that his region is the only place in the world where true tupelo honey is made (and that there are haunting, magnificent tupelo swamps on the east coast of Florida). What makes tupelo honey so pure and aromatic is that the bees rely exclusively on perfumey tupelo flowers for pollination.

A simple glazed ham is one of those classic dishes that has existed for generations for a reason. It's salty, sticky sweet, and meaty—what's not to love about digging into one? I generally reserve this dish for the holidays, but every now and then I'll break it out on a cool fall day with some mashed potatoes and green beans.

TUPELO HONEY– GLAZED
Ham

SERVES 8 TO 10

¼ cup packed light brown sugar
1 cup tupelo honey
½ teaspoon coriander seeds
½ teaspoon ground cloves
½ teaspoon ground cinnamon
½ teaspoon ground nutmeg
½ teaspoon cayenne
1 (5-pound) cooked boneless ham

Heat the oven to 350°F.

Heat the sugar, honey, coriander, cloves, cinnamon, nutmeg, cayenne, and ½ cup water in a medium saucepan over medium heat just until the sugar dissolves. Remove from the heat and let cool.

Put the ham in a roasting pan and spoon some of the sugar mixture over the top, until well coated. Don't use all of it, as you will be repeating this process every 10 to 15 minutes during the baking process. Bake the ham, basting regularly, until the meat has an internal temperature of 140°F and is coated with a thick dark amber glaze, 45 minutes to 1 hour.

Transfer the ham to a serving platter and tent with foil. Pour any remaining glaze into the roasting pan. Heat on the stove over medium-low heat, gently whisking, until everything that was baked onto the dish dissolves into the glaze. Simmer until syrupy, 4 to 5 minutes.

Slice the ham and serve with a generous drizzle of the reduced glaze.

I'VE LEARNED FROM my travels that "Milanese" is found not only in Milan, but is a cooking style used all over Europe. It's an especially great technique when dealing with tougher, drier cuts of meat like pork cutlets. A wet coating of mustard, lemon, and olive oil binds the bread crumbs to the meat, and lends a considerable amount of flavor to the dish.

Although this dish is fairly simple and straightforward, you need to pay attention to the details. Make sure you don't smear too much mustard on the pork, or the bread crumbs will slide off, and be sure to press the bread crumbs into the coating. When it comes to cooking, the heat needs to be medium-high, and the oil slightly smoking, before you add the cutlets. If it's not hot enough, the bread crumbs will stick to the skillet and really frustrate you. Finally, don't crowd the pan, and add oil as needed throughout the cooking process—this will help create the crispest crust and prevent the bread crumbs from burning.

CRISPY PORK CUTLETS
with Brown Butter, Lemon, and Sage

SERVES 4

1¾ pounds pork loin, cut into 8 equal pieces, each pounded ¼ inch thick

2 tablespoons kosher salt

¼ teaspoon black pepper

5 tablespoons Dijon mustard

About 1¼ cups olive oil

2 tablespoons fresh lemon juice

4 cups panko (Japanese bread crumbs)

3 tablespoons unsalted butter

1 tablespoon chopped fresh sage

1 teaspoon minced garlic

Season the pork with the salt and pepper. Combine the mustard, 3 tablespoons of the olive oil, and 1 tablespoon of the lemon juice, and coat both sides of each piece of pork. Pack the bread crumbs onto the coated pork, pressing down to ensure they stick.

Put a wire cooling rack inside a baking sheet.

Cook the pork cutlets in batches. For each batch, heat 3 tablespoons of the oil in a large skillet over medium-high heat, swirling to coat the pan. Just as the oil begins to smoke, add 4 pieces of pork. Add 2 more tablespoons of the olive oil and cook the pork until lightly browned, about 2 minutes. Flip the cutlets and add 3 more tablespoons of the olive oil. Cook for another 2 minutes. Transfer the cutlets to the wire rack.

Wipe out the skillet and return to medium-high heat. Add the butter and allow it to sizzle and brown. Add the sage, garlic, and remaining 1 tablespoon lemon juice and stir to combine. Transfer the pork to a serving platter and pour the sauce over the cutlets.

NOTE: Panko, or Japanese bread crumbs, vary in size. If they appear too coarse to coat the meat, pulse them finer in a food processor, or put them in a large zipper-top bag and crush them with a rolling pin to a finer grind. Don't go so far as to make fine crumbs, however; you want some texture here.

ONE SUMMER MY family and three of our friends decided to rent a house in the Languedoc for a couple weeks and explore the wines and food of southwest France. Of course, my first goal was to find cassoulet, the hearty bean- and meat-studded dish the region is famous for. When we arrived at the house we'd rented, weary after quite a long journey, we discovered a surprise from our host: a huge, beautiful cassoulet that was warm and ready to eat.

I had eaten cassoulet before, but never in France. Tasting the dish prepared with distinctively local ingredients, I learned another lesson: A recipe can have the same ingredients on paper, but taste a million different ways depending on the quality of what goes into it, and where you eat it. Luckily there is plenty of great sausage in the South, and this version yields entirely satisfying results. Cook this dish slowly and uncovered; if it cooks too fast, the beans won't have the silky creaminess that makes cassoulet so spectacular.

PORK BELLY *and* SMOKED SAUSAGE *Cassoulet*

SERVES 8 TO 10

1 pound dried white beans
(Great Northern or cannellini)

2½ pounds fresh pork belly, cut into
1½-inch cubes

2 tablespoons kosher salt

1 tablespoon black pepper

1 pound smoked sausage, cut into
2-inch segments

4 cups diced onions

2 cups diced celery

2 cups diced carrots

8 garlic cloves, minced

5 bay leaves

1 teaspoon red pepper flakes

1 teaspoon chopped fresh thyme

½ cup white wine

1 tablespoon tomato paste

3 tablespoons whole-grain mustard

About 2 quarts chicken broth

Put the beans in a large pot and cover with cold water by 6 inches; soak overnight and then drain.

Season the pork belly cubes with 1 tablespoon of the salt and 2 teaspoons of the pepper. Heat a large pot, preferably cast iron, over medium-high heat.

Heat the oven to 250°F.

Sear the belly pieces in batches, rolling them around in the pan to brown evenly on all sides, about 10 minutes per batch. Transfer the browned cubes to a plate lined with paper towels.

Sauté the sausage in the rendered belly fat until lightly browned, 2 to 3 minutes. Add the onions, celery, carrots, garlic, bay leaves, red pepper flakes, and thyme plus the remaining 1 tablespoon salt and 1 teaspoon pepper. Sauté until the vegetables start to soften, about 5 minutes. Pour in the wine and simmer to slightly reduce, about 3 minutes. Add the tomato paste and mustard and cook, stirring, until the ingredients are evenly combined, 2 to 3 more minutes.

Return the seared pork belly and any accumulated juices to the pot. Add 1 quart of the chicken broth and bring to a slow simmer, then cover, and simmer for 60 to 70 minutes. The belly will be cooked and slightly tender, but should not be falling apart.

Add the beans and remaining 1 quart broth, or enough to comfortably cover the beans by 2 inches. Put in the oven and bake, uncovered, stirring the top crust into the beans every hour or so, until the beans are tender, about 3½ hours. Add a little more broth if needed to keep the beans moist and submerged.

Increase the oven temperature to 450°F. Cook for another 30 minutes to form a crust on top of the bean mixture. Push the crust into the middle of the pot. Cook for another 15 minutes to form a new crust. The cassoulet will have a deep brown crust and look rich and delicious. Cool for at least 30 minutes before serving.

THIS FRESH, DEEPLY flavored recipe is an example of the new style of Southern cooking—global techniques applied to great local ingredients. The two-part cooking method, slowly braising the meat and then crisping it up to add another flavor dimension, is similar to the one used to make carnitas.

This dish is salty and rich, with bits of meat and counterpoints of bright flavors and texture. This method is perfect for shoulders and legs, which take some finessing to become tender.

I like to make the sauce with mint from my garden and goat's-milk yogurt from Bill Ryal, a goat farmer I met at the Crescent City Farmer's Market (where he sells goat meat and cheese). Over time, Bill and I talked about raising pigs. We made a deal: If he started raising pigs, I would buy them all. He called my bluff and now we buy all of our whole pigs from him.

BRAISED and CRISPY GOAT
with Yogurt Sauce, Cucumbers, and Mint

SERVES 4 TO 6

3 pounds goat or lamb shoulder

1 tablespoon plus 2 teaspoons kosher salt

1 teaspoon ground cumin

1 teaspoon black pepper

5 tablespoons olive oil

1 onion, diced

3 carrots, diced

4 garlic cloves, thinly sliced

1 cup dry white wine

1 tablespoon dried oregano

2 lemons, sliced into ½-inch rounds

½ cup plain whole-milk yogurt

Juice of 1 lemon, or more if needed

1 medium cucumber

1 cup fresh mint leaves, torn

1 head romaine lettuce

To prepare the goat, use a sharp knife to remove the sinewy silverskin from the shoulder, then cut the meat into 2-inch cubes. Combine 1 tablespoon plus 1 teaspoon of the salt, the cumin, and pepper in a bowl and then toss the seasonings with the meat until it is evenly coated.

Heat 2 tablespoons of the oil in a large skillet over medium-high heat. When the oil is hot, sear the meat in batches, so you don't crowd the pan, until well browned on all sides, 7 to 8 minutes. Resist the temptation to stir the meat too often or it won't brown properly. Transfer the meat to a plate.

Add 1 tablespoon of the oil to the skillet, then add the onion, carrots, and garlic, and cook, stirring occasionally, until soft, about 5 minutes. Add the wine and bring the mixture to a boil. Reduce the heat to low and simmer until the liquid is reduced by half. Add the oregano, lemon slices, and 6 cups water and bring the mixture to a simmer. Cover and cook over low heat until the goat is completely tender, about 2 hours.

Strain the mixture, reserving the sauce, and transfer the meat to paper towels to dry. Return the cooking liquid to a medium saucepan, bring to a boil over medium heat, and then simmer over low heat until slightly thick (there should be about ½ cup).

To make the yogurt sauce, combine the yogurt, lemon juice and remaining 1 teaspoon salt in a medium bowl. The mixture should be thin enough to drizzle (if it's not, add a bit more lemon juice or water).

Peel and dice the cucumber. Set aside.

When you're ready to serve, heat the remaining 2 tablespoons oil in a large skillet over medium-high heat. Sear the meat on all sides, until crispy and well browned, about 5 minutes. Transfer the meat to a plate lined with paper towels to drain.

Slice the romaine into ¼-inch ribbons and spread over the bottom of a serving dish. Top the lettuce with the seared goat meat and diced cucumber. Spoon the yogurt sauce and cooking liquid over the meat and garnish with the mint.

HEADS, FEET, NECKS, *and* BONES

Herbsaint Headcheese 114

FRIED FISH COLLARS
WITH CHILE VINEGAR 117

Breakfast Sausage 118

SAVORY SAUSAGE
AND CHEESE ROLLS 119

Pork Rillons 120

RICH PORK AND
CORNMEAL TAMALES 123

Fried Country Terrine 126

GUANCIALE 128

Brined Fresh Ham 129

TURKEY NOODLE SOUP 130

Pork Neck Bone Stew 132

MONDAY RED BEANS
AND RICE 133

Spaghetti with Pork Jowls
and Fried Eggs 134

BEEF SHORT RIB SUGO 137

Crispy Lamb Neck 138

The flavor of a boneless chicken breast will never be as good as that of chicken cooked on the bone. It's really that simple. Bones have flavor, make great sauces and stocks, and keep meat moist while it cooks.

Food prepared with bones, scraps, and animal heads may be too much for some people, but for me it's the highest echelon of enjoyment. What's more, using lesser parts of an animal is also a resourceful, responsible, and economical way to cook. At my house, if I roast turkey, I use the scraps for turkey stew; if I roast chicken, I immediately make stock with the carcass and vegetable scraps, which in turn I use to create another dish.

Not everyone knows what to do with these cuts, and many people don't want to know. I've been on thousands of fishing trips in my life, and I've rarely seen anyone bring home anything but the fillets. The exceptions are a Greek friend of mine who saved the heads for his mother to make fish head lemon soup, and a woman in Florida who saved them for fried fish collars. As much as I love a nice clean fish fillet, I'm a sucker for mullet throats in Alabama, whole fried flounder, whole grilled fish, and most of all, whole fried bluegills from Southern lakes, the best fried fish in the world (especially when fried in a cast-iron skillet at your fish camp). When I'm in Europe, it's whole grilled sardines and anchovies, which make some Americans squeamish.

One reason we don't see much of this in our food today is because the prime cuts come neatly packaged for us at the grocery store. When's the last time anyone cut up a whole pig? Head meat terrines are still pretty popular where I come from, and the French and Italians are extremely fond of them as well, but these cuts have never really made it into mainstream American eating. Years ago I began using whole pigs, lamb, and fish at the restaurant for a number of reasons, but mainly because there is so much flavor to be had from the "scraps," including in sausage, sauces, and crispy seared bellies.

You'll find a feast of options from unlikely sources in this chapter. Some of the recipes will require getting creative with your sourcing—connecting with a producer at your local farmer's market, for instance. But the resulting flavor will be well worth the effort—not to mention give you serious culinary street cred when you serve, say, Herbsaint Headcheese (page 114) or Crispy Lamb Neck (page 138) at your next cocktail party.

I KNOW THIS dish as headcheese, which is what it's called in Louisiana, but it can also be called a terrine or pâté, if you (or your guests) prefer. I've had versions of this recipe all around the world, from Alabama to Italy. On the west bank of New Orleans, the Vietnamese serve it on bahn mi sandwiches—one of my personal favorite uses for it.

Pigs are amazing—there really is no other animal that offers up so much of itself to enjoy. The recipe that follows is a pretty straightforward French preparation, although it's a time commitment: It takes a week to prepare. But the resulting flavors and textures—rich, decadent, and satisfying—are totally worth it. Serve this headcheese with mustard and crackers and anything pickled. It also makes a great sandwich on a baguette with mustard.

HERBSAINT HEADCHEESE

MAKES ONE 9 × 4-INCH LOAF

TO BRINE:

8 cups kosher salt

8 cups packed light brown sugar

4 onions, diced

10 jalapeños, halved

4 cups garlic cloves, smashed

3 bunches fresh thyme

2 bunches fresh flat-leaf parsley

2 cups fennel seed, toasted and cracked or partially ground

2 cups black pepper, toasted and cracked or partially ground

2 cups red pepper flakes

25 grams curing salt (see Note, page 44)

Head from a 210-pound pig, including some of the neck

At least 2 trotters

TO BRAISE:

½ cup vegetable oil

4 onions, diced

4 carrots, diced

2 heads celery, diced

1 cup garlic cloves, smashed

1 (750-ml) bottle dry white wine

2 bunches of fresh thyme

1 cup bay leaves

2 tablespoons red pepper flakes

4 quarts chicken broth

TO SEASON:

½ cup pickled mustard seeds (see Note)

2 bunches of fresh flat-leaf parsley, stemmed, leaves thinly sliced

8 jalapeños, stemmed, seeded, and finely chopped

Brine the pork: In a very large pot, bring to a boil 2 gallons water and all of the brine ingredients except the curing salt, head, and trotters. Boil for 10 minutes to allow the flavors to meld. Pour into a large bucket or cooler and add 2 gallons of ice. Add the curing salt and stir well to combine. Put the head and trotters into the brine. Fill a small kitchen-size trash bag with ice and use it to keep the head cold and submerged. Cover and brine in a cool place (like a cold garage), replacing the ice a couple times a day, for 6 days.

Remove the head and trotters, transfer to another large pot, and cover with water (discard the brine). Bring to a boil, then shut off the heat, remove the pork, and discard the water. Return the pork to the pot (or put it in a deep braising pan) and set aside.

Meanwhile, start the braise: Heat the oil in a very large Dutch oven over medium-high heat. Add the onions, carrots, celery, and garlic and cook, stirring, until softened, about 15 minutes. Add the wine and simmer to reduce by half. Add the thyme, bay leaves, and red pepper flakes and stir to combine. Pour in the chicken broth, bring just to a boil, and then remove from the heat.

Heat the oven to 200°F.

Pour the braising mixture over the pig head and trotters. It should only partially cover the pork (you want part to stick up out of the braise to caramelize in the oven). Cook the head in the oven slowly until completely falling apart, overnight or for 8 to 10 hours.

Carefully remove the head and trotters from the braise. Set aside to cool slightly. Strain the liquid into a large pot and skim off some of the fat. Simmer the braising liquid over medium heat to reduce until you see a large number of small bubbles, 15 to 20 minutes. Spoon some of the liquid on a cold plate in the freezer and allow it to cool completely—it should be the consistency of firm gelatin.

Meanwhile, pick the meat from the head, neck, and trotters, discarding any fat or sinew. Chop the meat into different sizes, cutting most of the meat into small pieces, while leaving some in large chunks.

Season the meat: Mix the meat with the mustard seeds, sliced parsley, and jalapeños. Add enough of the reduction to completely moisten the mixture. It should appear very juicy.

Line a 9 × 4-inch loaf pan with plastic wrap. Pour the pork mixture into the pan. Refrigerate overnight (or for up to 1 week) to allow the mixture to set up. Slice and serve.

NOTE: To pickle mustard seeds, soak them in red wine vinegar for 1 hour and then drain.

IN SOME PARTS of the Gulf Coast, these crispy meaty delicacies are also called fish throats, which is how they were listed the first time I ordered them. They're also found at my favorite sushi restaurants, where you can find hamachi and salmon collars on the menu. I can't believe that most fishermen and seafood markets dispose of them; given the choice, I'll take collars over the fillet all day long.

For the best flavor, the collars should be super fresh (ideally right off the fish you've just caught) and from larger fish, over four or five pounds. If you remove them yourself, I recommend using a pair of scissors to cut the collar away from the head after it has been removed from the rest of the body. The collars are a bit difficult to remove, just to warn you, but of course so is dissecting a fish head. I promise it's worth it. Scaling is optional, although I think the flavor and texture are more appealing with the scales off.

To eat these after they are fried, I strongly suggest just using your hands to tear into everything that's not bone. The fish fins fry nicely into crispy fish "chips" and are another delicacy to enjoy.

FRIED FISH COLLARS
with Chile Vinegar

SERVES 2

2 (8-ounce) fish collars
½ cup all-purpose flour
½ cup fine white cornmeal
1 cup buttermilk
1 tablespoon kosher salt
1 teaspoon black pepper
½ teaspoon cayenne
½ teaspoon paprika
Vegetable oil, for frying
Easy Pickled Chile Vinegar
(page 169)

Make sure the collars are dry before you start working with them; if they are wet, the batter will get clumpy and thick.

Combine the flour and cornmeal in a pie tin or wide mixing bowl. Pour the buttermilk into a wide, shallow container. In a small bowl, mix together the salt, black pepper, cayenne, and paprika.

Fill a pot large enough to hold the two fish collars with about 5 inches of oil and heat to 350°F.

Season the collars with the spices and let them sit for 2 minutes to allow the seasonings to settle onto the fish. Dredge the collars through the buttermilk and then in the cornmeal mix.

Put the collars in the hot oil and cook, flipping as needed, until crisp and golden brown, about 7 minutes. Use tongs to transfer to a plate lined with paper towels to drain any excess oil.

At this point I usually add a sprinkle of salt, but that's a personal preference. Then go ahead and get messy—dip the fish into a bowl of the chile vinegar and eat with your hands.

I KNOW IT may be hard to believe, but I do try to watch what I eat. In my attempt at virtue, I've learned that I have three major food weaknesses—hamburgers, Chinese food, and breakfast sausage.

I don't eat sausage for breakfast every day, but there are certain mornings when I desperately crave it (and that usually has something to do with what I did the night before).

If you have leftover sausage or just want to make it ahead of time, you can roll the mixture into a 2- to 3-inch cylinder in plastic wrap and freeze it. When you're ready for a hearty breakfast, just let it partially defrost, so it's still a little icy and easy to slice into rounds, and then fry.

BREAKFAST
Sausage

SERVES 6 TO 8

2 pounds ground fatty pork

1 tablespoon kosher salt

1 teaspoon black pepper

1 teaspoon cayenne

5 garlic cloves, minced

2 teaspoons chopped fresh sage

½ teaspoon red pepper flakes

¼ teaspoon ground allspice

2 tablespoons light brown sugar

2 tablespoons maple syrup

About 2 teaspoons vegetable oil or bacon fat

Combine all of the ingredients except the vegetable oil with ¼ cup water in a large mixing bowl (or the bowl of an electric mixer fitted with the paddle attachment). Stir to combine and then form into ¾-inch-thick patties.

To cook the sausage, heat a couple teaspoons of oil in a skillet (you just need enough to lightly coat the pan), preferably cast iron, over medium-high heat, and swirl to coat. Fry until browned and just cooked through, 2 to 3 minutes per side.

NOT ALL GAS stations in Louisiana sell these hearty, savory rolls, but there are some really good spots off I-10 selling greasy, spicy versions that are totally worth a detour. These rolls hold up well over time, making them perfect for road trips, picnics, ball games, and potlucks.

SAVORY SAUSAGE *and Cheese Rolls*

MAKES 10 ROLLS

1½ pounds loose pork sausage
1 large onion, cut into small dice
5 stalks celery, cut into small dice
3 garlic cloves, minced
1 teaspoon chopped fresh thyme
1 teaspoon kosher salt
½ teaspoon black pepper
¼ teaspoon cayenne
4 to 5 tablespoons panko (Japanese bread crumbs)
¼ cup plus 1 tablespoon sliced scallions
¼ cup plus 1 tablespoon thinly sliced fresh flat-leaf parsley
Yeast Roll dough (see page 60)
10 ounces white Cheddar cheese, shredded (about 1½ cups)
Butter, for greasing the pan
1 large egg, beaten

In a large skillet, sauté the sausage over medium heat, breaking it up with a spoon, until almost fully cooked, about 5 minutes. Add the onion, celery, garlic, thyme, salt, black pepper, and cayenne and cook until the vegetables are completely soft and lightly caramelized, 5 to 7 minutes. If the mixture starts to stick to the bottom of the pan, add a little water.

Remove the pan from the heat and add the bread crumbs, scallions, and parsley. Allow the mixture to cool completely.

While the sausage cools, portion your dough into ten 2½-ounce pieces and roll into individual balls. Cover the dough with a kitchen towel and allow the dough to rest for about 30 minutes. Flour a cutting board and use a rolling pin to roll the balls into 3-inch circles.

Add the cheese to the sausage mixture, using your hands to work it into the other ingredients. Divide the mixture into 10 equal portions.

Heat the oven to 400°F. Butter a baking sheet.

To fill the rolls, cup a circle of the dough in an upturned hand. Put a portion of the filling in the depression and wrap the dough around it. Twist the end in a circle until the dough breaks. This will form the bottom of your bun. Put the roll, seam-side down, on the baking sheet.

Whisk together the egg and 2 tablespoons water. Brush the rolls with the egg wash and bake until golden brown, about 15 minutes. Cool slightly; serve warm or at room temperature. The rolls will hold at room temperature for a few hours; after that wrap them in plastic and refrigerate for up to 3 days.

OF ALL THE terrine-style pork dishes, rillons, or slow-cooked cubes of pork rendered into a succulent spread, top my list because the flavors are unbelievably rich and satisfying. I like keeping the larger pieces of pork in the terrine because they add such luxurious texture. The recipe calls for pork belly, but any fatty scrap from the hog will work in this recipe.

My favorite way to eat rillons is on a crusty piece of bread as a sandwich with Creole mustard and nothing else, except maybe a little sprinkle of sea salt or a slice of pickled okra just to send it really over the top.

PORK
Rillons

SERVES 6 TO 8

2½ pounds pork belly, cut into 1-inch cubes

1 tablespoon kosher salt

¼ teaspoon cayenne

1 teaspoon black pepper

1 teaspoon curing salt (see Note, page 44)

1½ cups rendered lard or duck fat, plus more as needed

2 cups chicken broth, or as needed

2 shallots, diced

1½ tablespoons chopped fresh thyme

1½ tablespoons chopped fresh flat-leaf parsley

¼ cup cornichons, chopped

¼ cup cornichon juice

1 tablespoon fresh lemon juice

2 tablespoons Dijon mustard

Season the cubed pork belly with the salt, pepper, and curing salt. Refrigerate for 3 hours or overnight. Heat the oven to 500°F. Put the belly on a roasting rack above a roasting pan. Roast until the belly is nicely browned and caramelized, 20 to 30 minutes.

Lower the oven temperature to 300°F.

Remove the rack, tipping the pork cubes into the roasting pan. Add the lard and chicken broth to cover. Cook until the pork is completely tender, about 3 hours.

Using a slotted spoon, separate the meat from the braising liquid. Divide the meat into two equal portions; set aside. Put the roasting pan over medium-low heat and simmer the braising liquid until the bubbles come very quickly and most of the liquid has cooked away, about 12 minutes. Be careful not to burn the remaining fat. Remove from the heat and let cool partially.

Put half of the pork mixture in a mixing bowl. Using two forks or your hands, finely shred the meat. Stir in the shallots, thyme, parsley, cornichons, juice, lemon juice, and mustard. Slowly pour enough of the reduced fat mixture over the shredded pork to make it very juicy. Gently fold in the remaining half of the pork belly, keeping the cubes as intact as possible. Fold in more reduced fat as needed to keep the mixture moist.

Line a 9 × 5-inch loaf pan with a sheet of plastic wrap so that the edges hang over. Use a spatula to transfer the pork mixture to the pan. Wrap with plastic and refrigerate overnight (or for up to 1 week). Slice and serve.

MISSISSIPPI IS KNOWN for its tamales, and so is Zwolle, Louisiana, where the annual Tamale Festival is held every year. These are not your typical tamales; they are generally made with ground beef and lots of spices, rolled in parchment paper squares, stuffed into a wide can, and cooked in their own grease. They're something everyone should have at least once.

I've tried several methods of making tamales, including one from a Mexican woman in Veracruz, another from a Honduran woman, and of course, the Mississippi Delta variety. In the end I like my own improvised technique, which is simpler and more consistent. Tamale recipes traditionally call for corn masa, but we use Anson Mills coarse white cornmeal because it has an amazing corn flavor and wonderful coarse texture.

Once you've mastered the pork variety, be sure to try the shrimp variation; the addition of dried shrimp really intensifies the flavor.

RICH PORK and CORNMEAL *Tamales*

SERVES 10 TO 12

24 corn husks

3 cups white cornmeal, or more if needed (see Note)

3 cups masa

1 tablespoon plus 1 teaspoon kosher salt

½ cup rendered lard

6 cups chicken broth, hot

½ recipe Pork Rillons (page 120)

Prepare a steamer. Soak the corn husks in hot water until supple, 20 to 30 minutes.

Combine the cornmeal, masa, and salt in a large mixing bowl. Use your fingers to work the lard into the cornmeal until the mixture is coarse and pebbly. Stir in the hot broth.

To stuff the tamales, drain 1 corn husk at a time and shake off excess water. Put ½ cup of the cornmeal mixture in the middle of the husk, spreading it thinly. Put 2 tablespoons of the pork, with some of its juice, in the middle of the cornmeal mixture. Roll the husk into a long cylinder, then tie one end closed with kitchen string, and neatly fold the other end closed. Repeat with the remaining cornmeal and pork filling (you should get about 2 dozen).

Put the tamales in the steamer vertically, tied-end down, and steam until the cornmeal is firm and the filling is cooked through, 45 minutes. Serve hot.

NOTE: I've found that various brands of cornmeal thicken differently (some require more moisture than others to firm up). It's important to note that the finished consistency of the tamale dough should be fairly wet, yet thick enough to wrap around the meat filling. If the dough appears too liquidy, stir in a little extra cornmeal until it pulls together and feels right.

Delta Shrimp Tamales

SERVES 6 TO 8

3 tablespoons vegetable oil

4 cups chopped, peeled shrimp (about 3 pounds medium shrimp)

½ cup dried shrimp (available at ethnic and gourmet markets)

2 jalapeños, stemmed, seeded, and minced

½ medium onion, minced

1 tomato, diced

3 garlic cloves, minced

2 teaspoons kosher salt

1 teaspoon paprika

1 teaspoon ground cumin

1 teaspoon red pepper flakes

1 cup chopped fresh cilantro (leaves and tender stems)

Heat the oil in a large skillet over high heat. Add the shrimp, dried shrimp, jalapeños, onion, tomato, and garlic and cook until the shrimp release their liquid, about 4 minutes. Add the salt, paprika, cumin, and red pepper flakes. Reduce the heat to medium and simmer until the liquid is reduced to halfway up the ingredients, 5 to 7 minutes. Stir in the cilantro and follow the instructions on page 123 for filling and cooking the tamales.

TERRINES ARE A brilliant way to transform various scraps from a pig—from the neck, belly, shoulders, ribs, and so on—into something luxurious. Obviously you don't have to fry this terrine: It's delicious served in a traditional fashion with crusty bread, pickled vegetables, and mustard. But in the end, the Southerner in me needed to take the porky goodness to the next level, so I went for it.

The hot, crunchy crust and mustardy coating transform this rustic terrine into something totally different and delicious. Serve it alongside Sweet and Sour Spring Onions (page 193), Mustard-Marinated Turnips (page 192), and a handful of seasonal greens.

FRIED COUNTRY
Terrine

SERVES 6 TO 8 AS AN APPETIZER

2 cups small cubes of country bread

1 cup whole milk

1 tablespoon unsalted butter

1 medium onion, finely diced

4 garlic cloves, minced

1 tablespoon kosher salt

½ teaspoon red pepper flakes

½ teaspoon black pepper

2 tablespoons brandy

1 (2¼-pound) pork shoulder, cut into small dice (see Note)

½ cup chicken livers, cut into small dice

2 tablespoons Creole mustard

⅛ teaspoon curing salt (see Note, page 44)

1 cup Dijon mustard

3 tablespoons fresh lemon juice

1 cup panko (Japanese bread crumbs)

Olive oil, for panfrying

Combine the bread and milk in a mixing bowl and soak, stirring occasionally, until the bread starts to break down, 20 to 30 minutes.

Heat the oven to 300°F.

Melt the butter in a medium skillet over medium heat. Add the onion, garlic, salt, red pepper flakes, and black pepper and cook, stirring, until the onion starts to soften, about 4 minutes. Add the brandy and allow it to reduce slightly, about 2 minutes. Remove from the heat and let cool slightly.

In a large bowl, combine the vegetable mixture with the pork, chicken livers, Creole mustard, and curing salt. Add the soaked bread mixture and stir to combine.

Line an 8 × 4-inch loaf pan with parchment paper so that the edges hang over. Press the terrine mixture into the pan and cover it with the overhanging paper. Put the loaf pan in a large roasting pan and add water to come halfway up the sides of the pan. Bake in the water bath until the terrine's internal temperature reaches 150°F, about 1½ hours.

Remove from the oven and let cool slightly. Cut a piece of cardboard to fit inside the loaf pan and wrap it in plastic. Put the cardboard on top of the terrine and weight it down with can of beans or a wine bottle. Put on a rimmed baking sheet and refrigerate overnight.

The next day, invert the pan, using the plastic wrap to help unmold the terrine. Slice into ½-inch-thick slices. In a shallow bowl, whisk together the Dijon mustard and lemon juice. Spread the panko on a plate. Dip each slice of terrine into the mustard mixture and then press into the bread crumbs.

Heat 2 tablespoons oil in a large skillet over medium-high heat. Gently put 3 or 4 slices of terrine in the pan (as many as it can hold without crowding) and fry until golden brown on both sides, 3 to 4 minutes per side. Repeat with the remaining slices. Serve immediately.

NOTE: It may help to chill the pork almost to freezing before you cube it.

I HAD MY first taste of guanciale, a peppery, Italian-style bacon, at Salumeria Biellese in New York City. Being somewhat of a bacon fanatic, I was thrilled to find a new style of cured pork. Since I started making it myself, I've discovered that you should not overcook guanciale until it's super brown and crisp. Undercooking it slightly, so it's still chewy, allows more of the aromatics and natural hog flavor to come through.

Guanciale is great for giving long-simmered beans a different flavor than traditional bacon. It's also delicious with pasta and gnocchi, and it makes a mean BLT. It is probably best known for its use in carbonara, the famous pasta dish composed of hot noodles tossed with uncooked egg yolks, Parmesan, and black pepper.

GUANCIALE

MAKES 5 POUNDS

½ cup kosher salt

2 tablespoons black peppercorns, cracked

15 whole cloves

5 juniper berries, cracked

5 allspice berries, cracked

2 teaspoons red pepper flakes

1½ teaspoons ground nutmeg

1½ teaspoons curing salt (see Note, page 44)

4 garlic cloves, crushed

2 (750-ml) bottles of dry red wine

5 pounds whole pork jowls

Combine the kosher salt, peppercorns, cloves, juniper and allspice berries, red pepper flakes, nutmeg, curing salt, garlic, and red wine in a deep plastic container large enough to hold the pork. Add the jowls and toss briefly to combine (they should be completely covered), cover, and refrigerate for 2 weeks.

After 2 weeks, drain and rinse the jowls. Put them on a wire rack set over a baking sheet and allow them to air-dry, uncovered, in the refrigerator for another 3 days. At this point, the guanciale is ready to cook. Double wrap in plastic, in one-pound portions, what you are not using immediately and freeze until needed.

BUTCHERING A HOG and preserving the meat through cures, brines, and smoking was traditionally done to extend the shelf life of the meat and feed a family or a community by using as much of the animal as possible. In that spirit, Cajun boucheries were community gatherings that brought people together to celebrate the hog by making different preparations with each part of the pig. The same celebrations were (and continue to be) held in Europe. Since it's rather unlikely that you'll find yourself at a rural hog slaughter, try this recipe to make the most of a fresh ham leg—available at any good meat market.

BRINED
Fresh Ham

SERVES 15 TO 20

2 cups kosher salt

1½ cups packed light brown sugar

¼ cup red pepper flakes

3 tablespoons black peppercorns

2½ tablespoons allspice berries

2 tablespoons juniper berries

1½ tablespoons cayenne

1 tablespoon whole cloves

10 bay leaves

2 onions, sliced

2 carrots, sliced

2 celery stalks, sliced

1 bunch of fresh flat-leaf parsley

1 bunch of fresh thyme

3 tablespoons curing salt (see Note, page 44)

1 bone-in fresh ham (20 to 25 pounds), or 3 bone-in pork shoulders

Fill a very large (2-gallon or larger) pot with 1½ gallons water. Add the salt, brown sugar, red pepper flakes, black peppercorns, allspice and juniper berries, cayenne, cloves, bay leaves, onions, carrots, celery, parsley, and thyme and bring to a boil. Reduce the heat and simmer for 10 minutes to combine the flavors. Let cool slightly.

Transfer the brine to a large cooler and add 1½ gallons ice to quickly cool the mixture. Add the curing salt and stir well to combine.

Draw the brine into an injector (you can find these easily online) and shoot it into the ham every inch on the top and bottom. The brine will fill the ham and shoot out in different directions, so it's a good idea to do this in the cooler that you will store the ham in. After injecting, submerge the ham in the remaining brine. Fill zipper-top plastic bags with ice to keep the ham cold and submerged. Cover the ham and brine it in a cool place (like a garage or basement), replacing the ice a couple times a day, for at least 5 days and up to 8 days.

Set up your grill or smoker for low-and-slow cooking with wood chunks (see page 68).

Air-dry the ham for 1 hour, then put it on the grill, close the cover, and smoke at 225°F for 15 to 20 hours, until the internal temperature reaches 160°F. (If you want the ham to pull apart, cook it to 185°F.) Add more hot coals and a few wood chunks every 30 minutes or so, and adjust the vents as needed to maintain a steady temperature. There is no need to turn the ham.

Alternatively, you can cook the ham in a large roasting pan in a 225°F oven until it reaches an internal temperature of 160°F, 8 to 10 hours (or overnight).

EVERY YEAR I make this delicious, soothing soup the day after Thanksgiving. After everyone has had their fill of roast turkey and dressing, I wrap up the white breast meat for sandwiches and save the carcass and leftover dark meat for soup. The next morning it all goes into a large pot, with aromatic vegetables, to make a rich, fragrant broth. The big pot of soup sure comes in handy when we have extended family visiting, because it's so nourishing and it feeds a crowd. This soup is also proof that turkey is one of the most economical meats you can buy.

It's worth it to begin with the whole carcass (as opposed to turkey parts), and all the delicious pan drippings (those are the best reason to roast a turkey, in my book). When you add in the earthy flavors of the livers, neck, and gizzards, you end up with a rich, hearty soup.

TURKEY
Noodle Soup

SERVES 10 TO 14 (6 QUARTS)

TURKEY STOCK

Bones, wings, carcass, and pan drippings from 1 roasted turkey

1 onion, diced

2 celery stalks, diced

1 carrot, diced

4 bay leaves

1 tablespoon black peppercorns

SOUP

1 tablespoon olive oil

1 onion, diced

4 celery stalks, diced

2 carrots, diced

6 garlic cloves, minced

6 bay leaves

2 tablespoons whole-grain mustard

2 tablespoons red wine vinegar

1 tablespoon dried oregano

½ teaspoon poultry seasoning

Kosher salt and black pepper

2 to 3 cups shredded or diced turkey meat, preferably dark

8 ounces flat noodles (such as pappardelle or egg noodles)

Chopped fresh flat-leaf parsley, for garnish

Make the turkey stock: In a large pot, combine the bones, wings, carcass, and pan drippings (skimmed of fat) from the turkey with the onion, celery, carrot, bay leaves, peppercorns, and 6 quarts water. Bring to a boil over medium-high heat, then reduce the heat, and simmer, skimming the broth as needed, for 3 hours. Strain the stock. You need 4 quarts for this recipe; let any remaining stock cool before covering and refrigerating for several days or freezing for longer storage.

Start the soup: Heat 2 teaspoons of the olive oil in a large, heavy-bottomed pot or Dutch oven over medium heat. Add the onion, celery, carrots, garlic, and bay leaves and cook until the vegetables have softened, 5 to 7 minutes. Add the mustard, vinegar, oregano, poultry seasoning, 1 tablespoon salt, and 2 teaspoons pepper. Pour in the turkey stock and add the turkey meat. Simmer, skimming the fat as it rises to the surface, until the meat is very tender, 30 minutes to an hour.

When the soup is nearly ready, bring a large pot of water to a boil, season with salt, and add the noodles. Cook according to package directions until al dente. Drain the noodles and add them to the soup, simmering for 15 minutes to allow them to absorb the broth.

Taste for seasoning, adding more salt and pepper as desired. Serve the soup in wide, shallow bowls topped with chopped parsley.

ALSO CALLED BACKBONE stew, this is one of the most famous backwoods Cajun dishes in Louisiana. In Southwest Louisiana you can still buy meaty neck bone cuts at the grocery store. This is one of my favorite dishes to cook when I go home to Lake Charles, or I'm cooking for some Cajun home cooks or hunters. This is the food I was born to make: I can prepare it with my eyes closed. The fatty meat on the bone really does all the work. All I have to do is make sure it cooks slowly, allowing the flavors to develop and the meat to become silky tender.

PORK NECK BONE
Stew

SERVES 6 TO 8

1 tablespoon kosher salt

1 tablespoon paprika

2 teaspoons dried thyme

2 teaspoons cayenne

1½ teaspoons black pepper

1 teaspoon white pepper

3 pounds pork neck bones

⅓ cup plus ¼ cup all-purpose flour

Scant cup vegetable oil

1 pound smoked sausage, cut into
   ½-inch pieces

2 small onions, diced

4 celery stalks, diced

1 poblano, stemmed, seeded,
   and diced

1 jalapeño, stemmed, seeded,
   and minced

4 garlic cloves, minced

3 cups chicken broth

6 bay leaves

Steamed white rice, for serving

Combine 2 teaspoons of the salt, the paprika, thyme, cayenne, black pepper, and white pepper in a bowl to form a spice mix. Reserve 2 teaspoons of the spice mix and use the rest to season the necks. Then toss the necks with ¼ cup of the flour in a large mixing bowl until evenly coated.

Heat the oil in a large Dutch oven over medium-high heat and fry the necks until nicely browned, about 5 minutes per side. Transfer to a platter. Add the remaining ⅓ cup flour to the pot and cook, whisking constantly, to make a dark brown roux, about 25 minutes.

Add the sausage, onions, celery, poblano, jalapeño, garlic, remaining spice mix, and remaining 1 teaspoon salt. Cook, stirring, for another 5 minutes over medium-high heat. Pour in the chicken broth. Bring to a boil and then reduce the heat so the mixture simmers. Add the pork necks and bay leaves. Cook over very low heat until the pork necks are very tender and the sauce is a nice gravy consistency, 3 to 3½ hours. Add a little water if necessary while cooking if the liquid is reducing too quickly.

Serve immediately in wide, shallow bowls (discard the bay leaves) over hot steamed white rice.

RED BEANS AND rice has always been a New Orleans tradition on Mondays, and I can't think of a better way to kick off a week. Most agree that the custom started as a way to use up the leftover ham from Sunday night's dinner. My own personal red beans and rice tradition is to take my kids to the Louisiana Swamp Exhibit at the Audubon Zoo to watch the alligators, and order the red beans and rice they serve at the café there. I know it sounds crazy, but they're my favorite in New Orleans—perfectly creamy and delicious.

Let the beans take their sweet time to soften slowly and evenly while they absorb the ham and sausage flavor. The beans actually need to overcook a bit and break down to make the rich, thick "sauce" that partners so well with the fluffy rice.

MONDAY
Red Beans and Rice

SERVES 6 TO 8

1 pound dried red beans

1 large, meaty ham bone

6 bay leaves

½ pound smoked sausage, such as andouille, chopped into ½-inch dice (a generous cup)

½ pound smoked ham, chopped into ½-inch dice (a generous cup)

1 medium onion, diced

1 small tomato, diced

2 jalapeños, stemmed, seeded, and finely chopped

6 garlic cloves, finely chopped

2 tablespoons Creole mustard

¼ cup red wine vinegar

Scant tablespoon kosher salt

2 teaspoons dried thyme

½ tablespoon black pepper

1 teaspoon cayenne

Steamed white rice, for serving

Sliced scallions, for garnish

Hot sauce

Put the dried beans in a large pot of water (the beans should be covered by at least 4 inches of water). Soak the beans overnight and then drain.

Combine the beans, 1 gallon plus 2 cups water, the ham bone, and bay leaves in the same pot and bring to a simmer over medium heat.

Meanwhile, in a large skillet, cook the sausage and ham over medium-high heat until crispy and brown, 4 to 5 minutes. Add the onion and cook until softened, 5 minutes more. Add the tomato, jalapeños, garlic, mustard, vinegar, salt, thyme, black pepper, and cayenne and continue to cook until the mixture is hot and the ingredients have softened, an additional 5 to 8 minutes.

Scrape the sausage mixture into the pot of beans. Simmer slowly, uncovered, until creamy and tender, 2½ to 3 hours. Approximately 10 minutes before the beans are done, use a wooden spoon or spatula to smash some of the beans against the inside of the pot. If the beans are too firm, add a bit more water and cook until tender.

Serve over hot steamed white rice with sliced scallions and hot sauce.

THIS MAY BE the absolute most famous dish at Herbsaint, the one that can never, ever come off the menu. When I first developed this recipe, my intent was not to create a riff on pasta carbonara, but I immediately noticed the similarities. Instead of tossing the pasta with a raw egg yolk, I thought it would be cool if the egg yolk could run into the pasta at the table. It's blown a lot of people's minds since then.

As soon as the white of the egg is solid enough to remove from the water, lift out the egg and plunge it into ice water to stop the cooking. The eggs must be cold when they are fried or they will overcook. If your panko is too coarse, pulse the crumbs in a food processor for few seconds.

SPAGHETTI
with Pork Jowls and Fried Eggs

SERVES 4

4 large eggs
½ cup distilled white vinegar
8 ounces dried spaghetti
Vegetable or peanut oil, for frying
4 ounces pork jowls, diced (½ cup)
1 garlic clove, minced
¼ cup chicken broth
1½ cups heavy cream
1 cup all-purpose flour
1 cup buttermilk
1 cup panko (Japanese bread crumbs)
Kosher salt and black pepper
2 teaspoons thinly sliced fresh
    flat-leaf parsley
1 tablespoon fresh lemon juice
½ teaspoon red pepper flakes

Fill a wide 2-quart saucepan with about 4 inches of water. Add the vinegar and bring the water to just below simmering. Prepare a bowl of ice water. Crack each egg into a small cup and slip it into the hot water; cook until the whites are just set, about 3 minutes. Use a slotted spoon to transfer the eggs to the ice water. Transfer the cooled eggs to a shallow dish lined with paper towels (or a dish towel) and refrigerate for 30 minutes.

Bring a large pot of salted water to a rolling boil. Add the pasta and cook according to package directions, until al dente but not mushy; drain the noodles in a colander.

Meanwhile, heat 4 inches of oil in a medium pot to 350°F.

In a large skillet, cook the pork jowls over medium-high heat, turning as needed, until their fat has rendered and they are just starting to crisp, about 6 minutes. Add the garlic and cook for 1 minute. Pour in the chicken broth and heavy cream and simmer to reduce until the sauce is thick enough to coat the noodles, 5 to 6 minutes.

Put the flour, buttermilk, and panko in separate wide, shallow bowls. Dredge the eggs in the flour. Gently shake off the excess and dip in the buttermilk and then coat in the bread crumbs.

Deep-fry the eggs until nicely browned but still soft in the middle. Transfer to a paper towel, season with salt and pepper, and reserve.

Add the pasta to the sauce and toss to coat. Finish with the parsley, lemon juice, and salt and pepper to taste. Toss until combined and heated through. Divide the pasta among serving plates, sprinkle with a pinch of red pepper flakes, and top each with a fried egg.

WHEN BUYING SHORT ribs for this Italian-style meat sauce, look for ones that are cut across the bone; they'll deliver the most flavor. (Some are cut in between the bones, which isn't what you want here.) This is also good made with any fatty beef scraps, like chuck roast or rump roast.

Dried morels (available at any gourmet retailer) can be expensive, but they do make this dish special. You can substitute regular mushrooms like portobello or cremini, but double the amount and roast the mushrooms in a little oil in a hot oven first, to deepen their woodsy flavor.

This meat sauce makes for a lusty meal—serve it over egg noodles, pappardelle, polenta, or steamed rice with a voluptuous Italian red wine.

BEEF SHORT RIB
Sugo

SERVES 6 TO 8

5 pounds bone-in beef short ribs, cut into 2-inch pieces

Kosher salt and black pepper

Olive oil

1 onion, diced

10 garlic cloves, thinly sliced

4 plum tomatoes, diced medium

1 teaspoon dried oregano

1 cup dry red wine

1 quart chicken broth

1½ cups dried morels

Heat the oven to 400°F.

Generously season the short ribs with salt and pepper and lightly coat with olive oil. Put the ribs in a large, heavy-bottomed pot or Dutch oven. Roast in the oven until the meat is crusty and looks like the outside of good roasted prime rib, about 1 hour.

Add the onion, garlic, tomatoes, oregano, wine, broth, and morels to the pot and bring to a simmer over medium heat. Cover and simmer over low heat until the meat is very tender, 1½ to 2 hours.

THE FIRST THING you have to do to make this recipe is find some lamb necks. I would suggest starting at a farmer's market, if you have a local lamb farmer. If he doesn't have any on hand, he can probably save some for you for his next trip to the market. Chances are you'll find a source—just about everywhere that I've traveled in the South has a local lamb rancher.

There is a surprising amount of meat on a lamb's neck, and it's by far the most succulent part of the whole animal. It will likely take you two days to do this recipe, from start to finish.

CRISPY
Lamb Neck

SERVES 4

4 lamb necks, about 14 ounces each

4 tablespoons olive oil

1 tablespoon ground fennel seed

1 tablespoon red pepper flakes

Kosher salt and black pepper

2 onions, diced

2 large carrots, diced

1 fennel bulb, diced

4 celery stalks, diced

1 (750-ml) bottle of dry red wine

2 quarts chicken broth, or more if needed

5 bay leaves

2 (4-inch) rosemary sprigs

½ bunch of fresh thyme

2 tablespoons black peppercorns

Red wine vinegar

Vegetable oil, for frying (optional)

Put the lamb necks in a large bowl and toss with 2 tablespoons of the olive oil. Mix together the fennel seed, red pepper flakes, 1 teaspoon salt, and 1 teaspoon black pepper. Season the necks with the spice mixture. Marinate, uncovered, in your refrigerator overnight.

The next day, heat the remaining 2 tablespoons olive oil in a roasting pan over medium heat. Add the onions, carrots, fennel, and celery and cook, stirring, until they are soft and caramelized, about 20 minutes. Pour in the wine and simmer until it's reduced by three-quarters. Add the chicken broth, bay leaves, rosemary, thyme, and peppercorns. Simmer for 5 minutes.

Heat the oven to 250°F.

Ideally, you want to put the necks on a cooking rack above the liquid, and then loosely cover the dish. This will ensure a moist cooking environment, as the steam will flavor and gently cook the meat. If you cannot use the rack setup, then simply put the lamb necks in the liquid, ensuring that it comes no more than halfway up the sides of the necks. Put the pan in the oven.

The cooking process will take a long time—anywhere from 6 to 8 hours depending on the size of the necks. Start checking them after about 5 hours, adding more liquid as needed. When the necks are entirely tender and pull away from the bone very easily, remove them from the pan. Strain the sauce through a fine sieve and discard the solids. Season with salt or vinegar as needed.

You can heat the necks back up by roasting them in the oven at 450°F for about 15 minutes, or until hot in the center, or you can deep-fry them in 350°F oil for 7 minutes. Serve with the cooking sauce poured over the top.

SEAFOOD
from the Gulf and South Atlantic

Crab and Spinach Dumplings 144

WATERMELON GAZPACHO
WITH CRABMEAT 147

Beach House Ceviche 149

SHRIMP AND CRAB
SPAGHETTI 150

Crawfish and Spring
Onion Gratin 152

SCALLOP CRUDO
WITH TOMATOES,
LEMON, AND BASIL 155

Grilled Scallops with Green
Garlic Butter 156

SMOKED MULLET DIP 159

Catfish Court Bouillon 160

NEW ORLEANS BARBECUE
SHRIMP 162

Royal Red Shrimp 165

HOT COAL-FIRED
ROYAL REDS 166

Stone Crab Claws with Easy
Pickled Chile Vinegar 169

SOFT-SHELL CRABS
MEUNIÈRE 170

Crisp Fried Frog Legs 171

BROILED FLOUNDER
WITH CHERRY TOMATOES
AND BASIL 175

Butter and Olive Oil–Poached Tuna
with Kumquats and Chiles 176

SALT-CRUSTED
RED SNAPPER 177

My introduction to Gulf seafood involved a lot of fishing and shrimping with my dad, grandad, and uncles. Back then, seafood was truly local and if you were cooking it, that meant you had caught it, or someone you knew had. Redfish, shrimp, blue crabs, oysters, flounder, speckled trout, drum fish, and soft-shell crabs are the main catches around here.

Moving out into deeper waters, you start getting into the sport fish—marlin, tuna, cobia, mackerel, and snappers. As you move east to Alabama and Florida, you start seeing mullet, an interesting fish that jumps pretty far out of the water. They are really only good to eat when you get to the coast around Gulf Shores, Alabama, and farther east, as they live on sandy bottom waters and taste clean—unlike the Louisiana mullet, which no one will touch.

There's a famous bar on the border of Alabama and Florida called the Flora-bama (see page 22). It's a classic beach bar that sees about two thousand people a night getting hammered, and then holds church service on Sunday. Yep, welcome to the South. It is most known for its mullet toss—a hundred thousand people from around the world converge on the beach to see how far someone can throw a mullet.

To find the old Gulf Coast, drive east and you'll see the high-rise condos of the family vacation destinations fade into another world. About thirty miles east of Panama City, you'll come to the town of Wewahitchka, home of the only true tupelo honey in the world. After miles of pine forest, you suddenly find yourself in a swampy area with large oaks, tupelo trees, and cypress, with Spanish moss hanging everywhere.

If the Mobile, Alabama, tunnel is the gateway to the Emerald Coast, then Wewahitchka is the gateway to the Forgotten Coast. From Port Joe to Apalachicola, you'll find old Florida, where stretches of land look like they did long before a real estate developer stepped onto the scene. You know all those shells you see in the souvenir shops? Well, this is where the live ones are. It's also where the best fresh scallops can be found.

The Gulf Coast is a different South. It's where Southerners go to cut loose and be themselves, and it's the home of some interesting people who live a life that revolves around the water. To quote our scalloping guide, Captain Brent, "If you don't like fishing, why would you live here?"

SWEET CRAB AND earthy spinach make an incredible combination. Panfried and served with a buttery sauce, these tender, rich-tasting dumplings make an elegant first course.

CRAB AND SPINACH
Dumplings

SERVES 4 AS A FIRST COURSE

1 pound crabmeat

Kosher salt

1 pound fresh spinach, cleaned

1 large egg

2 tablespoons all-purpose flour, plus more for rolling

¼ teaspoon cayenne

⅛ teaspoon ground nutmeg

⅛ teaspoon white pepper

Unsalted butter

Beurre Blanc (recipe follows)

Pick the crab free of shells at least twice.

Bring a large pot of salted water to a boil. Have ready a medium bowl of ice water. Add the spinach to the boiling water and cook until just tender and still bright green, about 1 minute. Drain and transfer to the ice bath. When cool, drain again; use your hands to squeeze out excess water.

Chop the spinach, transfer to a bowl, and gently fold in the crab, egg, flour, cayenne, nutmeg, white pepper, and 1½ teaspoons salt. Using your hands, form the mixture into small, wine-cork-size dumplings.

Heat a sauté pan over medium-high heat. Drop in a generous piece of butter, swirl the pan to coat, and allow it to foam. Roll the dumplings in a small amount of flour, shaking off excess, and cook as many dumplings as will comfortably fit in your pan, being careful not to crowd them. Cook until lightly browned, turning as needed, about 6 minutes. Use a slotted spatula to transfer the dumplings to a platter (or hold them in a low oven to keep them warm).

Finish the dumplings with a drizzle of beurre blanc and serve.

(recipe continues)

Beurre Blanc

MAKES ABOUT ½ CUP

1 cup dry white wine

¼ teaspoon kosher salt

12 tablespoons (1½ sticks) cold
butter, cubed

Squeeze of fresh lemon juice

1 tablespoon chopped fresh
flat-leaf parsley

Simmer the wine and salt
in a small, nonreactive
heavy saucepan until about
2 tablespoons of liquid remain.
Slowly whisk in 1 cube of
butter at a time, waiting to
add the next until each is
fully incorporated. Add the
lemon juice and parsley; serve
immediately.

DRIVING THROUGH THE South in the summer, you're pretty much guaranteed to see someone selling watermelons alongside the road. It's a spectacular sight, an overflowing mound of mouthwatering green-and-white striped melons in the back of a pickup, all promising sweet, refreshing relief from the scorching heat. Which is exactly what you need after standing in the baking hot sun fishing for crabs. Rich crabmeat and sweet melons are perfect complements to each other. This gazpacho is great as a cooling first course for an outdoor get-together, and is especially delicious when topped with fresh-picked crabmeat tossed in mayo and lemon.

WATERMELON GAZPACHO
with Crabmeat

SERVES 6 TO 8 AS A FIRST COURSE

GAZPACHO
4 cups chopped ripe tomato

4 cups diced watermelon

½ fennel bulb, diced small

½ small onion, diced small

3 jalapeños, stemmed, seeded, and chopped

¼ cup loosely packed torn mint leaves

¼ cup loosely packed torn basil leaves

¼ cup red wine vinegar

1 teaspoon fresh lemon juice, or more to taste

2 teaspoons kosher salt, or more to taste

2 tablespoons extra-virgin olive oil, plus more for drizzling

CRABMEAT
½ cup mayonnaise

Grated zest and juice of 2 limes

1 small jalapeño, stemmed, seeded, and finely diced

10 mint leaves, thinly sliced

½ teaspoon red pepper flakes

Pinch of kosher salt

Pinch of sugar

1½ pounds jumbo lump crabmeat

Make the gazpacho: Combine all of the ingredients in a blender. Blend on low to combine and then raise the speed to medium for a few pulses (the mixture should be evenly combined, but still a little chunky). Taste for seasonings and add more salt or lemon, as desired.

Carefully pick the crab free of shells—do this at least twice. Combine the mayonnaise, lime zest and juice, jalapeño, mint, red pepper flakes, salt, and sugar in a mixing bowl and then gently toss in the crabmeat.

To serve, divide the gazpacho among wide bowls. Divide the dressed crabmeat among the bowls and finish with a drizzle of olive oil.

SOMETIMES IT'S DIFFICULT for me to take super fresh seafood, straight from the water, and cook it. It just seems wrong not to enjoy the fresh, pristine flavor of the raw fish. Enter this ceviche.

A couple of years ago I was at a wedding in Cabo with my family. My son Nico and I decided we were going to have a boys' day. I called my friend Andrew Zimmern and asked where we should go to eat, and he recommended El Juanillo, a seafood joint. One of the brothers who owned the place prepared a delicious ceviche from an ice chest, on a cart on the sidewalk outside the seating area, with a steady stream of seafood brought to him by fishermen straight off the boats. It was so good, I ate there three times in four days!

This is my version, one that we scarf down with tortilla chips at the beach house in Florida. The chile powder, along with the sweetness of the vinegar, gives great balance to what I feel can sometimes be an overly acidic dish. The watermelon became our addition at Herbsaint: The sweetness really pulls all the flavors together.

BEACH HOUSE
Ceviche

SERVES 8 TO 10 (WITH DELICIOUS LEFTOVERS)

8 ounces grouper, cut into small dice

¼ cup plus 2 tablespoons muscadine or red wine vinegar

Juice of 2 lemons

8 large shrimp, cooked and diced (for cooking method, see page 52)

10 ounces sashimi-grade tuna, cut into small dice

1 cup diced watermelon

½ cup diced cucumber (see Note)

¼ cup finely chopped red onion

2 serrano chiles, stemmed, seeded, and minced

¼ cup chopped fresh cilantro (leaves and tender stems)

1 tablespoon pure ground chile powder (such as ancho or New Mexico)

1 tablespoon kosher salt, or more to taste

¼ cup extra-virgin olive oil

Give the grouper a head start by combining it in a medium bowl with the vinegar and lemon juice. Cover with plastic and refrigerate for 30 minutes, until it doesn't taste raw. Then transfer to a large bowl for mixing and add all of the remaining ingredients. Taste for seasonings and add more salt, as desired. Serve immediately.

NOTE: Peeling a cucumber lengthwise with a zester (the handheld kind usually used for lemons), as opposed to a vegetable peeler, leaves thin strips of the skin intact and really brings out its clean flavor.

I'VE OFTEN THOUGHT of certain foods as flavoring ingredients. Smoked ham hocks and bacon are perfect examples. In this case it's the shrimp heads and the crab fat and juice. When cooked down into a seafood broth—an essential layer of flavor in this recipe—they provide a deep, distinctive taste. This decadent tangle of spaghetti is luxuriously rich in crab: both meat foraged from the whole crabs and additional lump meat. The hot chiles elevate, brighten, and lighten the dish while pulling all the flavors together. This is just the kind of buttery dish that you want to dive into with after a day on a boat or the beach.

SHRIMP AND CRAB
Spaghetti

SERVES 4 TO 6

½ pound medium shrimp

3 medium blue crabs (this should yield an additional ½ pound lump crabmeat)

1 tablespoon olive oil

½ onion, chopped

2 bay leaves

1 (3-inch) rosemary sprig

Kosher salt and black pepper

1 pound dried spaghetti or cappellini

4 tablespoons (½ stick) unsalted butter

1 teaspoon minced garlic

1 jalapeño, stemmed, seeded, and minced

½ pound jumbo lump crabmeat

¼ cup chopped fresh flat-leaf parsley

2 tablespoons torn fresh basil

Peel the shrimp, coarsely chop, and reserve the shrimp and shells separately. Clean the crabs: Split each crab in half to open. Pull out the plate from underneath. Use your fingers to pull out the yellowish-orange fat from both sides of the back shell and reserve. Discard the lungs and the helmets (the back of the shell). Add any more crab fat (from both sides of the shell and the head area) to your stash. Pick the meat from the shell; you should have ½ pound. Reserve the meat, shells, and fat separately.

Heat the oil in a medium saucepan until hot and shimmering. Add the shrimp and crab shells, the onion, bay leaves, rosemary, and 1 teaspoon black pepper. Cook until the shrimp shells turn pink and all the ingredients are fragrant and coated with oil, about 3 minutes. Add 4 cups water and bring to a boil, then reduce the heat, and simmer until you have about 1 cup broth, 12 to 14 minutes. (You'll need ½ cup for this recipe; the rest freezes well.)

Bring a large pot of generously salted water to a boil. Cook the pasta according to package directions and drain.

Meanwhile, melt 2 tablespoons of the butter in a large skillet. Add the shrimp, crab fat, garlic, and jalapeño and cook until fragrant and sizzling, 3 to 5 minutes. Pour in ½ cup of the shrimp stock and the remaining 2 tablespoons butter to pull the sauce together. Add the lump crabmeat, parsley, and basil. Stir to combine and then toss with the cooked pasta. Serve immediately.

CRAWFISH SEASON IN Louisiana is at its peak in the spring. I look forward to this all year because it is the only time I eat them. You can find crawfish other times of the year that have been frozen for a long time or that come from China. Do not buy these; they are inferior in flavor and this dish will not taste good with them. My first preference would always be to peel my own crawfish to ensure that I get out all the fat, which is what really gives this dish its rich, decadent flavor. If you decide to go this way, realize that it takes seven or eight pounds of whole crawfish to get a pound of tail meat. If you are purchasing tail meat, buy Louisiana crawfish with as much fat in the bag as you can.

CRAWFISH
and Spring Onion Gratin

SERVES 6 TO 8 AS AN APPETIZER

4 tablespoons (½ stick) unsalted butter

2 cups thinly sliced spring onion bulbs

¾ cup diced celery

2 jalapeños, stemmed, seeded, and minced

2 garlic cloves, minced

2 scallions, sliced

2 teaspoons kosher salt

½ teaspoon black pepper

¼ teaspoon cayenne

1 pound crawfish tail meat (defrosted if frozen)

¼ cup dry white wine

2 tablespoons all-purpose flour

1 cup heavy cream

Squeeze of fresh lemon juice

1 cup grated white Cheddar cheese

⅓ cup grated Parmesan cheese

½ cup panko (Japanese bread crumbs)

Heat the broiler.

In a 10- or 12-inch cast-iron skillet, melt 2 tablespoons of the butter over medium heat. Add the onions, celery, jalapeños, garlic, scallions, salt, black pepper, cayenne, and crawfish and cook, stirring, until the vegetables soften, 4 to 6 minutes. Pour in the wine and continue to simmer until the liquid is reduced by two-thirds, about 4 more minutes. Add the flour and cook, stirring, until the mixture is evenly coated. Pour in the cream and simmer until reduced by about a quarter, about 5 minutes. Turn off the heat and stir in the lemon juice and both cheeses.

Melt the remaining 2 tablespoons butter and combine with the panko in a small bowl.

Transfer the crawfish mixture to a 6 × 8-inch baking dish, top with the bread crumbs, and broil until the crumbs are nicely browned, 1 to 2 minutes.

I HAVE TO be honest: I'd always thought of the Northeast and Taylor Bay (on Cape Cod) when it came to sweet, rich-tasting scallops. I just learned a few years ago that you can snorkel off the "lost coast" of Florida (an undeveloped section of coastline along the Panhandle) and forage for your own scallops.

The experience of snorkeling in three feet of water is quite interesting, kind of like a cross between snorkeling in the Caribbean and in Toledo Bend Lake in Louisiana. The water at first appears murky, but it's actually very clear with a dusty bottom of sea grass, which provides nice camouflage for the scallops that nestle there. Every once in a while, one of them surfaces and, via jet propulsion, rises from the grass and swims away, looking a bit like some crazy Millennium Falcon.

Let's be honest: Cleaning scallops is a good bit of work for a little bit of meat, but it's so worth it. I've always thought that certain foods have a "best" way to be enjoyed, and I think in the case of bay scallops, raw is the way to go. I'm particularly fond of this Italian method of serving fresh-from-the-water seafood, simply seasoned with citrus and salt.

To serve this dish, divide the marinated scallops among small plates, alongside baguette slices or tortilla chips.

SCALLOP CRUDO
with Tomatoes, Lemon, and Basil

SERVES 4 TO 6 AS AN APPETIZER

12 fresh bay scallops in their shells (or 1 pint shelled bay scallops)

1 medium ripe tomato, finely diced

Grated zest and juice of 1 lemon, or more to taste

1 tablespoon chopped fresh basil

1 tablespoon plus 1 teaspoon extra-virgin olive oil

½ teaspoon kosher salt, or more to taste

A few grinds of black pepper

Fill a sink with cold water and rinse the scallops, changing the water several times. Set up a bowl of ice water.

Use a knife to carefully open each scallop and trim away the connective tissue that holds the muscle to the shell. Trim the scallops of any grit and transfer to the ice water.

In a medium bowl, combine the tomato, lemon zest and juice, basil, olive oil, salt, and pepper. Transfer the scallops from the ice bath to a clean towel to dry, turning them to blot away any excess moisture. Add the scallops to the bowl with the tomato and use a large spoon to toss well. Taste and adjust the seasonings, adding more salt or lemon as desired.

Serve immediately, or chill the scallops for 30 minutes to allow the flavors to combine.

WHAT TO DO with fresh, beautiful scallops that you've just foraged from the bay? As little as possible. In this recipe, fresh scallops are cleaned and returned to their shells, which become a handy cooking vessel for a hot grill. The sweet scallops are crowned with a disc of spicy garlic butter. When the scallops sizzle over the heat, a buttery, oceany sauce forms in their shells. If you begin with ultrafresh scallops, these will likely be the best things you'll ever put in your mouth.

GRILLED SCALLOPS
with Green Garlic Butter

SERVES 4 TO 6 AS AN APPETIZER

2 tablespoons thinly sliced green garlic (or scallions)

1 garlic clove, minced

1½ tablespoons chopped fresh flat-leaf parsley

1 teaspoon kosher salt

½ teaspoon paprika

Generous pinch of cayenne

½ tablespoon hot sauce

Grated zest and juice of ½ lemon

8 tablespoons (1 stick) unsalted butter, at room temperature

24 bay scallops, in their shell

Put all of the ingredients except the butter and scallops in the bowl of a food processor and puree into a finely ground paste. Transfer the garlic mixture to a medium bowl and use a rubber spatula to combine with the butter. Shape the butter into a log, wrap in plastic, and chill until firm.

In the meantime, clean the scallops. Fill a sink with cold water and rinse the scallops, changing the water several times. Set up a bowl of ice water.

Use a knife to carefully open each scallop and trim away the connective tissue that holds the muscle to the shell. Trim the scallops of any grit and transfer to the ice water. Clean and save half of the shells, for grilling.

When you're ready to cook the scallops, heat your grill to medium.

Put the cleaned scallops, each in one of their half shells, on a rimmed baking sheet. Top each scallop with a generous teaspoon of the garlic butter. Grill the shells directly on the grill until the butter melts and starts to bubble and the scallops are just cooked through, about 3 minutes.

MULLET IS A delicious white fish with an unfortunate name (and, in modern vernacular, a reference to an unfortunate hairstyle). But along the Gulf Coast, it's embraced and celebrated. And no place reveres the humble mullet quite like the Flora-bama, the rough and rowdy beach bar that straddles the Alabama and Florida state lines (see page 22).

Mullet is a firm and slightly dry fish, so it benefits from a healthy dose of mayo and sour cream—which explains why smoked fish dips are a summer beach house staple along the Alabama and Florida coasts. Some of my favorites include those served at the Original Point in Perdido, Hunt's Oyster Bar in Panama City Beach, and Papa Joe's in Apalachicola. They are accompanied by saltines or tortilla chips, and garnished with a leaf of lettuce or an array of toppings (onions, fresh tomato, pickled jalapeños, shredded lettuce).

SMOKED MULLET *Dip*

SERVES 4 TO 6

2 cups smoked mullet or tuna,
  skinned and picked for bones

¼ cup diced onion

1 celery stalk, minced

2 scallions, thinly sliced

1 small jalapeño, stemmed,
  seeded, and diced

½ cup mayonnaise

½ cup sour cream

2 tablespoons Creole mustard

1 tablespoon prepared horseradish

1 teaspoon Worcestershire sauce

Finely grated zest and juice of
  ½ lemon, or more to taste

1 teaspoon hot sauce,
  or more to taste

1 teaspoon kosher salt,
  or more to taste

½ teaspoon black pepper,
  or more to taste

½ teaspoon paprika

Combine all of the ingredients in a mixing bowl, using two forks to shred the ingredients together into a coarse puree (for a smoother texture, pulse the ingredients in a food processor). Taste and adjust the seasonings, adding more lemon, hot sauce, salt, and pepper as desired. Transfer to a serving bowl and, for best results, cover and refrigerate for a few hours to allow the flavors to develop.

WHEN I OPENED a Cochon restaurant in the heart of Cajun country, I put this dish—my version of catfish court bouillon (aka coo-be-yon)—on the menu. I like it because it is light and tasty and easy to eat. Turns out there are a whole lot of versions of this recipe, and they are all the "real one" according to their devotees. From what I gather, what the "real one" entails is a roux and some canned tomatoes. I'm going to have to disagree with that. The best I can decipher from my research is that a true court bouillon is made with whole bone-in catfish or *gaspergou,* a swamp fish; covered with broth or water, peppers, onions, and tomatoes, and left alone to simmer; then served, bones and all. I've had it, and it's good. So anyway, catfish court bouillon is not the *Highlander* battle cry—there can be more than one.

CATFISH COURT
Bouillon

SERVES 4

1 tablespoon unsalted butter

½ medium onion, finely chopped

1 celery stalk, finely chopped

½ red bell pepper, finely chopped

1 medium tomato, diced

1 jalapeño or serrano pepper, stemmed, seeded, and finely chopped

4 garlic cloves, minced

½ teaspoon dried thyme

Kosher salt

White pepper

Black pepper

¼ teaspoon paprika

½ cup dry white wine

1½ cups seafood stock (see Note) or chicken broth

2 tablespoons vegetable oil or bacon fat

1 pound (3 or 4) skinned catfish fillets, cut into 4-inch pieces

½ cup all-purpose flour

½ cup cornmeal, preferably white and finely ground

¼ cup coarsely chopped fresh flat-leaf parsley

¼ cup chopped scallions

Juice of 1 lemon

5 basil leaves, coarsely torn

Hot steamed rice, for serving

Melt the butter in a large skillet over medium heat. Add the onion, celery, bell pepper, tomato, jalapeño, garlic, thyme, 1 teaspoon salt, ¼ teaspoon white pepper, ¼ teaspoon black pepper, and the paprika and cook, stirring, until softened, about 5 minutes. Pour in the white wine, bring to a boil, and simmer until it has almost completely evaporated, about 10 minutes. Pour in the stock and simmer 10 minutes more. Remove the skillet from the heat and cover to keep warm.

Heat the oil in a cast-iron skillet over medium-high heat. Season the catfish with salt and black pepper. On a plate or in a pie tin, whisk together the flour and cornmeal. Dredge the fillets in the

cornmeal mixture, shaking to remove excess, and transfer to the skillet, rounder side down. Cook until light golden, 3 minutes, then flip the fish, and add the sauce. Simmer until the fish is just cooked through, 5 to 8 minutes. Stir in the parsley, scallions, lemon juice, and basil.

To serve, spoon the rice into bowls. Gently remove the catfish with a slotted spatula and set over the rice. Spoon a generous amount of sauce over the catfish.

NOTE: Any type of seafood stock will work for this dish. I recently made this recipe with a crawfish stock, because I happened to have some on hand. Traditionally court bouillon is made with fish stock, but shrimp stock (see page 150), or virtually any shellfish stock, or even chicken stock, will work just fine. Do not, however, make this with water, because it won't be worth the effort, flavorwise.

WHEN I THINK about classic New Orleans dishes, this one is at the top of the list. It's messy in a completely fun, butter-bath kind of way. Don't make this dish if you don't have head-on, shell-on shrimp; it just won't be the same. There is some sort of magic created by having the heads on, and in the way the flavor melds with the butter and black pepper.

Reducing the stock with the lemon and Worcestershire creates an intense flavor foundation and also helps to emulsify the butter, instead of having a broken butter sauce.

NEW ORLEANS
Barbecue Shrimp

SERVES 6 TO 8 AS AN APPETIZER

1 teaspoon vegetable oil

1 pound jumbo (12-count) shrimp, shell and head on

2 (3-inch) rosemary sprigs

3 garlic cloves, sliced

Grated zest of ½ lemon

1½ teaspoons kosher salt

1 tablespoon black pepper

½ cup shrimp stock (see page 150)

2 teaspoons Worcestershire sauce

Juice of 1 lemon

8 tablespoons (1 stick) unsalted butter, cubed

1 loaf of French bread, toasted and sliced

Heat a skillet, preferably cast iron, over high heat until hot. Pour in the oil, swirl to coat, and then add the shrimp in an even layer. Add the rosemary, garlic, lemon zest, salt, and pepper, and cook, stirring occasionally, until fragrant.

Pour in the shrimp stock, Worcestershire, and lemon juice, flip the shrimp, and cook for 2 minutes more. Simmer the liquid to reduce by two-thirds.

Gradually add the cubed butter, stirring it into the sauce, and continue to cook until the sauce is shiny and thick, about 4 minutes. Serve with plenty of toasted bread for mopping up the buttery sauce.

WHEN I FIRST heard about Royal Reds, I didn't believe the hype. I couldn't imagine that they were that much better than the Gulf shrimp that I grew up on. But as much as I hate being wrong, they are. Most prominent near the Florida-Alabama border, Royal Reds are caught in waters offshore, in depths of over a thousand feet, making them really salty and sweet, similar to spot prawns from the Northwest.

There is no need to salt the water when cooking these. If you're brave enough, try eating the legs underneath the shrimp and the head underneath the outer shell: They are truly amazing. (I was at a lunch in Gulf Shores, Alabama, with some soccer parents during a tournament and when I explained how to eat these, everyone thought I was joking.)

The first place that I had these was the Original Point Restaurant in Perdido, Florida, an amazing old-school seafood restaurant. On one trip there, we discovered that they play bluegrass music from Thursday to Saturday, in the middle of the dining room. Put it on your list—the tunes plus these shrimp serve up the real Gulf South.

ROYAL RED
Shrimp

SERVES 4 TO 6

1 pound Royal Red shrimp, shell and head on

½ pound (2 sticks) unsalted butter

Grated zest and juice of 1 lemon

1 tablespoon Worcestershire sauce

2 garlic cloves, minced

1 (3-inch) rosemary sprig

½ teaspoon black pepper

¼ teaspoon cayenne

Bring a large pot of water to a boil, add the shrimp, and cook until bright pink and firm, 5 to 7 minutes depending on their size. Drain and transfer to a serving bowl.

In a medium skillet over low heat, combine the butter with the lemon zest and juice, Worcestershire, garlic, rosemary, black pepper, and cayenne. Heat just long enough to marry the flavors together, a minute or two. Pour the sauce into individual ramekins (discard the rosemary).

To eat, peel the shrimp and dip them into the butter sauce. Don't forget to eat the inner head and legs. To eat the legs, turn the shrimp over and bite them off like you would eat corn on the cob. Trust me.

YOU CAN USE any large Gulf shrimp in this recipe, although I think you'll get the best results with Royal Reds. I like this method for a couple of reasons. First, it's great when you're grilling other meats and want shrimp as well, because you can do it all on the same fire (just remember to clean the grill in between). Second, I like the way the smoke from the coals adds another dimension to the sweet flavor of the Royal Reds.

HOT COAL-FIRED *Royal Reds*

SERVES 4 TO 6

8 tablespoons (1 stick) unsalted butter, at room temperature

2 teaspoons minced garlic

2 teaspoons hot chili garlic paste (found in Asian markets)

Grated zest and juice of 1 lemon

Grated zest and juice of 1 lime

2 tablespoons coarsely chopped fresh parsley or cilantro leaves

1 pound Royal Red shrimp

1 tablespoon olive oil

Heat your grill to medium-high.

Use a whisk or a fork to combine the softened butter with the garlic, chili paste, lemon and lime zests and juices, and parsley in a mixing bowl. The butter should be soft enough to blend well without much effort, but it should not be runny, so that it will melt against the hot shrimp coming off the grill without breaking and getting greasy. If it gets too soft or looks broken, just put it in the fridge to firm up a bit, but don't take it back to cold butter consistency.

Toss the shrimp in the oil, and then grill until the shells take on a bright pink color, 4 to 5 minutes per side depending on the size and thickness of the shrimp. Toss the hot shrimp with the garlic chili butter, pass the napkins, and then peel and eat.

SWEET, RICH, AND beautiful, crab claws are one of the great luxuries of the Gulf Coast. They're traditionally served with tartar sauce, but I think bright chile vinegar is an even better complement. Stone crabs are sold at the best fish markets, steamed and cracked, which makes for an easy, elegant appetizer.

STONE CRAB CLAWS
with Easy Pickled Chile Vinegar

SERVES 4 TO 6

½ cup Easy Pickled Chile Vinegar (recipe follows)

Grated zest and juice of 1 lime

1 tablespoon chopped fresh cilantro

¼ teaspoon kosher salt

2 pounds cooked, cracked stone crab claws

Combine the chile vinegar with the lime zest and juice, cilantro, and salt in a small serving bowl. Serve the dipping sauce alongside a platter of cold stone crab claws.

Easy Pickled Chile Vinegar

MAKES ABOUT 3 CUPS

This quick method for pickling chiles will add a punch of flavor to countless dishes: vinaigrettes, tuna or chicken salad, fried chicken, fried shrimp, crab claws. It will last in your fridge for several months, if not longer. Banana peppers work particularly well because they're a nice, medium-heat pepper, hot enough to be interesting, but not so much as to be overpowering. The idea is to use a generous amount of the vinegar and chiles in a dish to add that pickled tartness.

2 cups sliced banana chiles, stemmed but not seeded

1 cup sliced serrano chiles, stemmed but not seeded

3 cups distilled white vinegar

¾ cup sugar

1 teaspoon kosher salt

Put the sliced chiles in a 1-quart glass jar. Bring the vinegar, sugar, and salt to a boil in a nonreactive saucepan. Cool briefly and then pour the hot vinegar over the chiles. Cool again for a few minutes, then cover with the lid and refrigerate for up to 3 months.

I DEBATED WHETHER to call for sautéing or frying in this recipe. If you are not in the mood to fry, then by all means coat the crabs in flour and sauté them. They'll be great—just not as great as they would be fried. I have done soft-shell crabs every way you can think of, but nothing, and I mean nothing, comes close to how good they are crispy and fried. I love a wet batter for these crabs, because it provides the perfect combination of crunchy fried stuff on the outside and juicy white delicious crabmeat inside. If you fry them whole, it's a perfect balance—the juice from the crab soaks into the fried crust.

SOFT-SHELL CRABS
Meunière

SERVES 4

BEER BATTER

1 cup rice flour

1 tablespoon all-purpose flour

About ¾ cup beer

1 teaspoon kosher salt

1 teaspoon black pepper

¼ teaspoon cayenne

Peanut or vegetable oil, for frying

4 large or 8 small to medium
   soft-shell crabs

1 teaspoon kosher salt

¼ teaspoon cayenne

Meunière Sauce (recipe follows)

Make the beer batter: In a medium bowl, whisk together the rice flour, all-purpose flour, beer, salt, black pepper, and cayenne. The batter should be thin enough to barely coat your fingers; this is not a heavy pancake batter.

Fill a medium pot with 3 inches of oil and heat to 350°F.

Cut the crabs into quarters (cutting in between the legs and across the body) if they're small, and 6 pieces if they're large; then season with the salt and cayenne.

Dip each piece of crab in the beer batter and fry until light golden brown, about 2 minutes. Do not crowd the pot. Transfer to paper towels to drain. Serve with the meunière sauce.

Meunière Sauce

MAKES ABOUT ⅓ CUP

2 tablespoons unsalted butter, cold

3 tablespoons chicken broth

2 teaspoons fresh lemon juice

1 teaspoon drained brined capers

½ teaspoon minced garlic

⅛ teaspoon red pepper flakes

Heat a small skillet over medium-high heat. When the skillet is hot, add 1 tablespoon of the butter and swirl to coat; when it starts to turn a golden brown, add the chicken broth, lemon juice, capers, garlic, and red pepper flakes. Slightly reduce the heat and then simmer to reduce by half. Remove from the heat and swirl in the remaining tablespoon butter. Serve hot.

I **LOVE FROG** legs and think they are one of the greatest indigenous Southern delicacies you can find—especially the frogs from Rayne. They are better than any I have had in France, and absolutely better than anything farmed in Asia. The meat is delicate, flavorful, clean, and unique. After tasting them, I vowed never to serve or eat imported frog legs again. Louisiana frogs ruined me forever.

But now that I understand *exactly* what is involved in procuring frogs, I understand why cheap imported frog legs are what most restaurants use. Chinese frog legs sell for $3 to $4 a pound; meaty Raynes go for $14 to $18 per pound. But I think you get what you pay for—or what you stay up all night frogging to catch!

CRISP FRIED
Frog Legs

SERVES 2 TO 4

8 (2-ounce) frog legs,
   with backs removed
Peanut or vegetable oil
1 tablespoon kosher salt
1 teaspoon black pepper
½ teaspoon cayenne
Beer batter (see page 170)

The trick to making good fried frog legs, especially with a wet beer batter, is to make sure the legs are really dry. Lay out the frog legs on paper towels and refrigerate for at least 30 minutes, uncovered, before seasoning and frying.

In a heavy pot, heat 4 inches of oil to 350°F.

Season the frog legs with the salt, black pepper, and cayenne. When you're ready to fry, dredge the legs through the beer batter, allowing excess batter to drip off, and carefully drop into the oil, being careful not to crowd the pot. Fry until a good golden crust forms, about 4 minutes. Transfer to paper towels to drain; serve hot.

My first attempt at catching a giant bullfrog did not work out so well. I was nine years old, at my grandad's camp at Toledo Bend, Louisiana, where, at the bottom of a slight hill, there was a small pond nestled between his place and the lake. I knew that the frogs came out at dusk, so that's when I planned to make my move. I crawled on my stomach through sticky weeds and moist grass, as quietly and slowly as possible, until I reached the crest of the hill, where I could see the pond. I peered down to spy about ten of the largest bullfrogs I had ever seen lounging at the edge of the water. When I say large, I mean at least ten inches wide *before* they are stretched out. I had no idea what I would do if I actually caught one, but I thought I needed some evidence—I figured no one would believe me if I told them what I had seen. When the time seemed right I moved slowly onto my feet so that I could creep toward the closest frog, sneak up on it—and grab it. But I wasn't halfway up before every one of them flopped into the pond, disappearing in a riot of splashes. Who would believe me now?

Flash forward thirty years to a June evening in Rayne, Louisiana, the self-proclaimed frog capital of the world. (They are not exaggerating—I've stood outside in Rayne when you could barely hear yourself think because the sound of millions of croaking frogs was so deafening. It's both cool and a little creepy.)

LEAP OF FAITH LATE-NIGHT FROGGING IN RAYNE

Until this night in early June, I had yet to be on an *official* frogging trip. Sure, I'd caught a few toads and frogs here and there, but I'd never been on a "let's get some frogs for dinner" type mission. Rayne used to be where four-star restaurants in New York would procure the meatiest and best-tasting frog legs for their menus. Then drastically cheaper varieties became available from China, imported frogs became the norm in restaurants, and the commercial industry here dried up. I wanted to see firsthand what the deal was, so I called my cousin Billy, a crawfish farmer from Rayne, and asked him if he knew someone who could take me out. That's when he told me how many fat bullfrogs he saw *daily* in the rice fields—a proposition I couldn't refuse.

The following weekend, Billy, a friend of mine, and I met up in the country to prepare. First off, we needed to get a few beers in us. We couldn't go out until nine or ten, when the frogs came out en masse, so we took the time to take the edge off. We got in Billy's crawfish boat with another case of beer and a giant floodlight and headed out into the rice fields, which were flooded with about a foot of water. This is when I discovered that you definitely *don't* want to be the person holding the floodlight. I've been around plenty of bugs and mosquitoes, but nothing like the swarm that consumes you when you are holding a bright light in a rice field in the middle of the night. The first hour we didn't see much of anything, except the beautiful red moon rising on the night horizon. The buzz of the boat motor drowned out any sounds from nature as we patrolled the banks of the fields looking for the telltale reflective light that frogs' eyes give off when the floodlight shines on them. Eventually and mysteriously, after more beer and more bullshit, I noticed that I could no longer hear the boat motor over the reverberating chorus of frogs. It was now midnight, and the sound of frogs had taken over the sound of the motor. It was time to get serious.

Most people "gig" frogs, which involves spearing and paralyzing them with a three-pronged spear, but we had decided that we were going to snatch them with our bare hands. At first, I didn't believe this was possible given my experience as a kid. The trick, I now learned, is to lean over the boat with your arm extended out, motionless, as you approach the glowing eyes. When you are in place, you slap the back of the frog the same moment that you grab it. This must be done in one confident swift motion. Even the slightest twitch will make the frog bolt into the water. Unless you're Billy, who can jump out of the boat and grab two frogs, one in each hand. I still don't know how the hell he does it.

For the next two hours we snatched frogs out of the water like wild Cajuns. By the time we had forty in the boat, held captive in mesh crawfish bags that had to be retied every time you put one in so they wouldn't jump out, I started to think about cleaning all those frogs the next day. And that's when I decided we had enough.

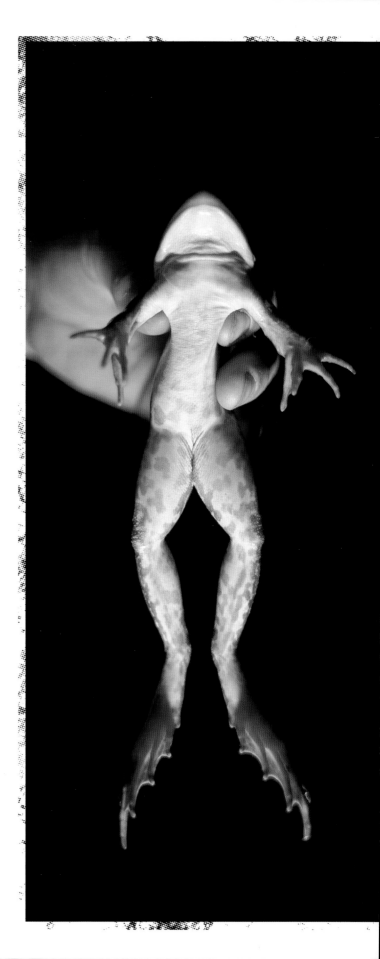

I LOVE THIS method of cooking thin, firmly textured fish such as flounder, trout, tilapia, and even smaller salmon. These fillets are generally less than half an inch thick, so they should be cooked quickly, using very high heat. You can use this same recipe for thicker varieties of fish, but cook them in a hot (475°F) oven instead of under the broiler; otherwise they will get too dark on top before they are cooked through. (Do the same if your broiling rack is fixed closer to the heat source than 6 inches.)

I've started preparing my fish at home this way fairly often, because it's quick and really lets the fish flavor come through; the results are both buttery and clean. It's also a great way to cook several fillets at the same time without using a lot of sauté pans. I find that pan-searing thin fillets can dry the outsides of the fish, whereas this method keeps them perfectly moist throughout. Consider serving this fish alongside buttered cappellini (or other pasta) or new potatoes and a simple arugula and Parmesan salad.

BROILED FLOUNDER
with Cherry Tomatoes and Basil

SERVES 4

4 (6- to 8-ounce) skinless fish fillets (such as flounder, trout, or tilapia)

1 teaspoon kosher salt

Black pepper

Pinch of cayenne

4 tablespoons (½ stick) unsalted butter, cut into ½-inch slices

2 tablespoons extra-virgin olive oil

Juice of 2 lemons

1 pint cherry tomatoes, halved

8 fresh basil leaves

Fifteen minutes before cooking, position a rack 6 to 8 inches below the heat source and turn on your broiler.

Season one side of each fillet with salt, a few twists of black pepper, and a tiny pinch of cayenne (pinch a little between your thumb and index finger and open them *very slowly* to release only a small amount).

Put the butter in a 9 × 13-inch glass baking dish and set in the oven to melt the butter, about 30 seconds. Remove the dish and add the olive oil, lemon juice, and tomatoes. Toss carefully to coat the tomatoes.

Lay the fillets with the seasoned side up in the baking dish and spoon some of the melted butter sauce on top. Work the cherry tomatoes in between the fillets so the fish isn't covered. Broil the fish until cooked through, 4 to 6 minutes. Test doneness by gently pushing the fish with your finger. If it springs back, it is not cooked; it should feel like it is giving slightly when you push on it.

Transfer the fish to serving plates. Tear the basil leaves into pieces with your fingers and stir them into the buttery sauce remaining in the baking dish. Spoon the sauce over the fish and serve immediately.

I KNOW A lot of people who go offshore fishing for tuna and as a result, I often get great high-quality tuna. Slow-cooking tuna in a fragrant citrus- and chile-infused olive oil bath softens the meat, giving it a unique tenderness and flavor while also keeping it very moist.

BUTTER *and* OLIVE OIL–POACHED TUNA *with Kumquats and Chiles*

SERVES 4 AS AN APPETIZER OR 2 AS A MAIN DISH

2 tablespoons unsalted butter

2 tablespoons extra-virgin olive oil

1 tablespoon fresh lime juice, preferably from Key limes

1 jalapeño, stemmed, seeded, and minced

4 kumquats, thinly sliced

2 (5-ounce) tuna steaks (2 to 3 inches thick)

6 fresh mint leaves, torn into small pieces

Warm the butter, olive oil, and lime juice in a medium skillet (large enough to hold the tuna in a single layer) over medium heat. Add the jalapeño, kumquats, and tuna. Shallow-poach the tuna for about 2 minutes on each side. You want to warm the tuna but not cook it. It should be rare when served.

Transfer the tuna to a cutting board and cut into ⅓-inch slices. Arrange on plates. Add the mint to the sauce in the pan and spoon over the tuna.

WHEREAS THE LOUISIANA coastal regions are known for redfish and speckled trout, the deep waters off the coast of Florida are famous for red snapper, an impressive, brightly colored reddish-pink fish that's a blast to reel in.

On a recent deep-sea fishing trip with a group of friends, I met a first-generation Italian cook named Maria who taught me this simple, delicious method for a salt crust, which has changed my approach to cooking whole fish. It's perfect for snapper—it keeps the fish incredibly moist and is practically foolproof. In fact, all of the food Maria prepared surprised me, from her herbaceous *salsa verde* (see recipe, page 179), a nice accompaniment to this dish, to crispy fried fish collars (see page 117). She expertly filleted a fish on the boat and prepared a quick crudo—raw snapper drizzled with oil and lime juice—along with a side of cucumbers to keep me from getting seasick. If that weren't enough, she also cleaned the fish with me back at the dock (although it was more like I helped her clean the fish).

SALT-CRUSTED
Red Snapper

SERVES 4 TO 6

2 pounds kosher salt
2 pounds rock salt
1 (4-pound) fresh snapper, gutted, head on
Best quality extra-virgin olive oil
Flaky sea salt, for serving

Heat the oven to 475°F.

Line a rimmed baking sheet with aluminum foil. Spread a layer of both salts on the foil. Put the snapper on top of the salt. Cover the fish with the rest of the salt, until you have a white mound enclosing the fish. Sprinkle a little water on top, enough so the salt feels like wet sand (you'll use anywhere from 2 to 3 cups). Use both hands to pack the salt around the snapper. It should be completely covered and sealed for the salt to bake into a tight dome and lock in the moisture.

Put the snapper in the oven and bake until cooked through, about 35 minutes (that's 10 minutes per pound for the first 2 pounds, then 7 to 8 minutes for any additional pounds). Remove the fish from the oven and allow it to rest for 5 to 7 minutes.

To serve the fish, crack the crust by gently piercing the center of the salt dome lengthwise with a knife, in ½-inch increments, being careful not to go too deep; you don't want to pierce the fish. Carefully pull the pieces of salt crust off in big pieces. Use a knife to carefully peel the skin from the fish (it will be very soft), and then use large forks or metal spatulas to transfer the fillets onto a serving platter, leaving the bones behind. Drizzle with your best-extra virgin olive oil, sprinkle with sea salt, and serve immediately.

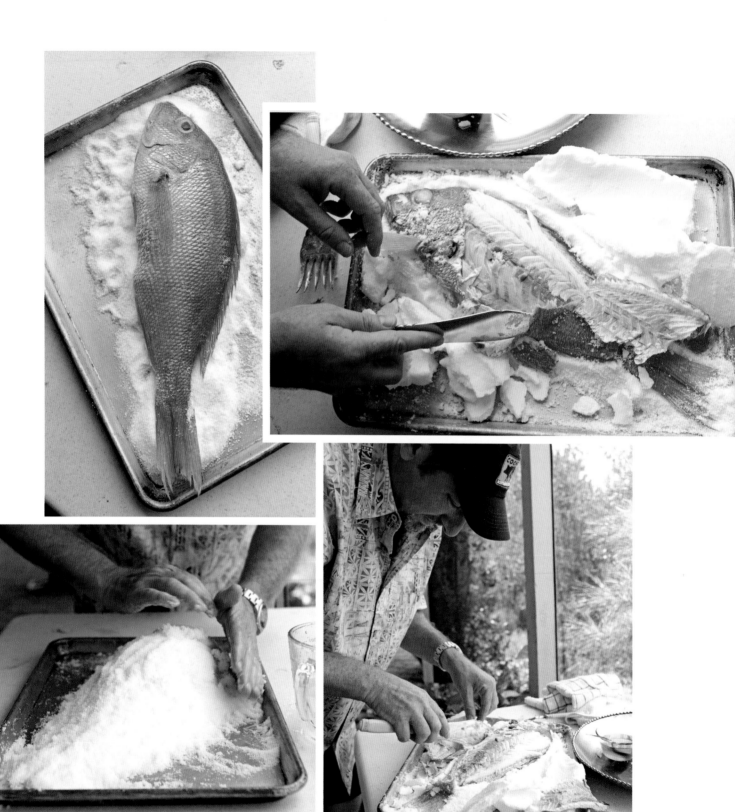

Salsa Verde

MAKES ABOUT 1¾ CUPS

This simple puree of garlic, herbs, and oil creates a fresh and vibrant condiment for any simply prepared fish.

3 anchovy fillets
2 garlic cloves
½ cup white wine vinegar
Grated zest and juice of
 1 lemon
1 tablespoon Dijon mustard
¾ cup extra-virgin olive oil
1 shallot, minced
½ cup chopped fresh flat-leaf
 parsley
½ cup chopped fresh mint
Kosher salt and black pepper
Red pepper flakes

Pound the anchovies and garlic with a mortar and pestle; transfer to a medium mixing bowl. Whisk in the vinegar, lemon zest and juice, and mustard. Add the olive oil in a slow, steady stream, whisking constantly. Stir in the shallot, parsley, and mint; add salt, pepper, and red pepper flakes to taste.

There are different ways to go about fishing. Some people, like my friend Dave Pasternak, the chef at Esca (a Southern Italian trattoria in New York City devoted to seafood), will fish anywhere, anytime, and in any weather. Now, I love to fish—a lot—but cold northern waters? You can have that; no thanks. I've fished for halibut in the icy waters near Bolinas, California, until I broke out into a cold sweat (the first sign before throwing up), and I've fished for salmon off the coast of Seattle. There aren't enough Windbreakers: It's too damn cold for this Southerner.

I guess growing up down here spoiled me, because when I think of fishing I imagine sparkling spring and fall days. Even on a sweltering summer afternoon, when you're on a pontoon boat, you can simply jump in the lake to cool off.

For me, fishing falls into three categories: lake, marsh, and deep-water Gulf fishing.

Bass fishing on a calm, glassy lake with my dad, while the sun is rising through the cypress trees and geese are flying low over the mist on the lake, is about as good as life gets. Our tradition is to get up quietly, so we don't wake the rest of the family, make coffee, grab some snacks, and head out just before sunrise, so we are cruising the banks just as the sky is starting to color.

I love all the sensory details of fishing: the solitude and the quiet; the aroma of coffee poured from a thermos; the murky, fertile smell of the moist morning air. In particular, I like the sounds: the lure whizzing through the air right before it splashes into the water, and the water in turn being split by the approach of the lure returning to the boat. There are different types of lures, but I mainly use two for lake fishing: the quiet plastic worm and the louder top-water bait. The latter makes a great noise on the lake, like a motorless steel propeller churning the still water, and it makes for some exciting fishing because the bass have to jump out of the water to catch it. Snagging one is always an unexpected, sudden, and thrilling moment.

A FEW WORDS ABOUT FISHING

When it comes to worm fishing, the idea is that you move the hooked bait slowly, in an up-and-down motion, to simulate a worm falling through the water. Once you get the "bump," as it's called, it's best to wait just a half second or so—but no more—before "setting the hook" by jerking the rod straight up.

Down South, the marshes are generally brackish, or a mix of fresh and salt water. The prize catches here are redfish, speckled trout, and black drum. Redfish are my favorite for their clean, full flavor and for the fun of catching them—they put up a better fight than the other varieties.

Marsh fishing calls for another early-morning departure. The water is shallow, and the bait of choice is a live shrimp cast with a cork on the line, a toss that requires a little skill to master, especially with four other people on the boat. (Marsh fishing is often a guided outing, and it's done in a larger boat with everyone standing.) Be careful when fishing with novices: You'll want to watch every cast they make, so you don't end up with a hook in your neck. It happens.

Another option on marshes is bow fishing, something that any sports enthusiast should try once. If you follow the river south, about forty miles from New Orleans you'll hit Woodland Plantation and Spirits Hall, a historic inn that offers guided fishing tours. This is where I start most if not all of my marsh excursions, especially the nighttime outings. We usually kick things off with drinks and dinner at Woodland; both the food and libations are incredible. Foster Creppel, the owner, likes to make a "SOCO," or Southern Comfort punch, for everyone—since the plantation is depicted on the bottle.

After a fifteen-minute ride with earmuffs (the fans on an airboat are pretty loud), we get to our spot and the driver cruises around the grassy islands. Rows of lights shine into the water from the boat and create an outline of the fish when they get within twenty feet. Bow fishing is not an easy endeavor. You need to hold the bow and arrow (which is attached to a string) at the ready position, all night. The fish swim by in a blink, and you have about three seconds to respond. I absolutely love this shit. Unfortunately, redfish over five or six pounds start to get tough, so as much fun as it is to snag the really big ones, they don't taste that good. The best-tasting fish are smaller and more difficult to hit.

Deep-water Gulf fishing is another deal entirely. The most exciting part of offshore fishing is that you are catching some really big fish, which are a blast to reel in. Tuna, cobia, mackerel, American red snappers, and large groupers are just a few of the varieties that flourish in the deep, cold water. Some of these catches might take well over an hour to reel in. The upside is that you will have more fish than you know what to do with. The downside is that you will be taking a boat twenty to fifty miles offshore, so depending on the weather and your proclivities toward seasickness, this could also be the worst day of your life.

Along the way (and thanks to some unfortunate expeditions—I'll spare you the details), I've learned some tricks to avoid getting seasick. First, get the patch and put it on the day before. When you're on the boat, don't stare at the horizon—that doesn't work. Do not drink beer if you are feeling queasy (this one was hard for me to accept). Do not go inside the boat to hang out or scare up some snacks. Instead, stay busy and focused on fishing and do not obsess about the state of your stomach. Another trick is to eat some cucumbers with salt; this works for me.

Once you get your land legs back, the olive oil–drizzled, sea salt–dusted feast that awaits (along with a river of cold white wine), and the stories and laughs that follow, usually obliterate the memory of the shaky journey. Which is why I keep going back for more. No matter where you ease your boat into the water, the important thing is to disconnect from your daily responsibilities, breathe in the moment, have fun, and enjoy the company.

Fresh, Seasonal SOUTHERN SIDES

Carrot Raisin Salad 186

GINGERED APPLE SLAW 188

Collard Green Slaw 190

SPRING PEAS WITH
FETA AND MINT 191

Mustard-Marinated Turnips 192

SWEET AND SOUR SPRING
ONIONS 193

Marinated Eggplant with
Chile Flakes and Mint 194

FRESH MINT COUSCOUS 195

Smoked Ham and Rice Salad 196

I-TALIAN STYLE BROCCOLI 198

Cajun Macaroni Salad 199

CAULIFLOWER AND GRUYÈRE
GRATIN 201

Ham Hocks and Crowder Peas 202

TASSO AND WHITE BEAN
GRATIN 204

Sweet Potato Gratin 205

In 2000 I opened Herbsaint in New Orleans after two three-year stints as a chef in San Francisco. I had become ridiculously spoiled by the endless bounty of beautiful fresh fruits and vegetables that are seemingly always available on the West Coast. When I returned to Louisiana and went to my first farmer's market, the contrast was shocking. I had grown up eating garden-fresh vegetables from my grandad's farm, so I knew the potential and variety of what could be grown, but I didn't see any of it in New Orleans.

At first I started to research how I could ship produce from California, because there is only so much you can do with zucchini and bell peppers. After struggling with shipping costs, I had another idea. I needed to make it attractive for farmers to grow for us at the restaurant. And that's when something incredible happened.

Thanks to an increasing number of restaurants demanding local ingredients, and to the work of Richard McCarthy at the Crescent City Farmer's Market, New Orleans has become a town brimming with luscious, great-tasting produce. There are now dozens of farms that grow specific varieties and quantities for my restaurant group all year long. What was missing when I returned to my home state—a direct connection between farmers and restaurants, as well as between farmers and other buyers and consumers—is now a robust exchange.

The difference between the carrots we were buying when we opened and the carrots we have now is so radical that the first specimens should not even have been called carrots. When preparing the recipes in this chapter, know that they will taste better if you rely on locally grown ingredients.

The vibrant possibilities in this chapter give vegetables the respect they deserve, and will help you plan meals around a host of seasonal options. Many of these recipes are hearty enough to make a meal, especially when paired with a green salad, some good bread, and a great bottle of wine. Don't be surprised if the meat winds up being an afterthought.

THIS DISH STICKS out in my mind as one of those classic Southern sides that somehow nobody ever thinks about but everyone likes. Made with freshly dug carrots and plump raisins, this staple can be an ethereal experience. The curry may seem unusual but works magically with the mayonnaise and other ingredients, as if it were always supposed to be there.

CARROT RAISIN
Salad

SERVES 4 TO 6

½ cup plus 2 tablespoons mayonnaise

2 teaspoons curry powder, preferably homemade (recipe follows)

2 teaspoons kosher salt

¼ teaspoon cayenne

Juice of 1 lemon

1 pound carrots, peeled and shredded (about 4 cups)

2 cups good-quality raisins

1 cup loosely packed fresh flat-leaf parsley leaves, thinly sliced

In a medium bowl, mix the mayonnaise with the curry, salt, cayenne, and lemon juice. Fold in the carrots, raisins, and parsley. Refrigerate for an hour or up to 4 hours to allow the flavors to develop.

Homemade Curry Powder

MAKES ABOUT ¼ CUP

I strongly encourage you to make this delicious curry blend, a recipe from my chef and business partner Ryan Prewitt. The flavors are warm and aromatic. Stored in a tightly sealed container in a cool, dark place, this blend will keep for several months.

2 teaspoons cumin seeds

2 teaspoons cardamom seeds

2 teaspoons coriander seeds

1 tablespoon plus 1 teaspoon ground turmeric

1 teaspoon dry mustard

Heaping ¼ teaspoon cayenne

Toast the cumin, cardamom, and coriander seeds in a small, dry skillet over medium-low heat until the seeds are lightly browned and fragrant, 2 to 3 minutes. Transfer to a bowl and let cool completely. Add the turmeric, mustard powder, and cayenne and mix to combine. Grind the spices in a coffee grinder. Store in an airtight container for up to 2 months.

AS A CHILD I had salads similar to this one, made with sugar, apples, and raisins. As I grew up, so did the South. I never saw cilantro and ginger as a kid, but these ingredients take what was a sweet, mayonnaise-soaked salad to a bright, modern, and exciting rendition. Generally speaking, when I think of apples I think of the Northwest—or rather, I did until I met Steve Vetter, one of our local farmers who drives to Georgia every fall to bring back crates of delicious Pink Lady apples. The best apples to use in this slaw are sweet, crunchy varieties; Gala, Braeburn, and Golden Delicious are other good options.

GINGERED
Apple Slaw

SERVES 4 TO 6

4 apples, cored and cut into matchsticks (about 4 cups)

½ cup mayonnaise

Juice 1 lemon

1 tablespoon ginger juice (see Note)

2 tablespoons chopped fresh cilantro leaves

1 large jalapeño, stemmed, seeded, and minced

Kosher salt and black pepper

2 ounces crispy prosciutto or country ham (optional; see Note)

In a medium bowl, use a rubber spatula to combine the sliced apples with the mayonnaise, lemon juice, ginger juice, cilantro, and jalapeño; season with salt and pepper to taste. Toss with the prosciutto, if desired.

NOTES: Ginger juice adds a spicy kick to vinaigrettes and sauces, especially creamy dressings that temper its sharpness. To make ginger juice, use a box grater or large-toothed Microplane to grate about 2 tablespoons of ginger. Then use your fingers to squeeze the juice from the grated pulp. Alternatively, you can use a garlic press to extract the pungent juice from a slice of fresh ginger.

If you want to add crispy prosciutto to the salad, thinly slice the ham and fry it in a couple tablespoons olive oil until crisp, about 3 minutes. Transfer to a plate lined with paper towels to drain. Break the ham into small pieces over the salad.

BELIEVE IT OR not, I had to go all the way to Seattle to figure out that collards can be cooked in a way other than smothered in bacon and onions. I had an incredible opportunity to cook on a small dairy farm off the coast of Seattle and create everything from the garden on the farm, which included some beautiful succulent baby collards. Now don't get me wrong: Bacon-braised collards are one of my most cherished childhood foods and one of the prime examples of real Deep South cooking. But these just didn't need as much help due to their size and sweet flavor. So I went a different route, opting to parblanch them and dress them with a spicy and sharp vinegar dressing.

COLLARD GREEN
Slaw

SERVES 4 TO 6

Kosher salt

1 large bunch of small, young collards

3 tablespoons good-quality red wine vinegar

1 tablespoon extra-virgin olive oil

Scant ½ teaspoon red pepper flakes

Bring a large pot of salted water to a boil. Have ready a bowl of ice water. Cut the leaves from the center stalks. Blanch in the boiling water until bright green and just barely tender, about 20 seconds. Scoop out and transfer to the ice bath. Once cool, drain thoroughly.

Cut the greens into ½-inch strips. Toss with the vinegar, olive oil, pepper flakes, and salt to taste. You can serve the slaw immediately, or let it marinate in the refrigerator for up to 4 hours so the flavors can combine.

IN THE EARLY spring when peas are fresh and sugary, shelling them yourself is totally worth the fuss. Mint and feta create a sweet-and-salty combination that's great with grilled fish or roasted chicken.

SPRING PEAS
with Feta and Mint

SERVES 4 TO 6

Kosher salt

3 cups shelled fresh English peas (from 2 pounds of pods)

¼ cup fresh mint leaves, torn

2 tablespoons extra-virgin olive oil

2 teaspoons fresh lemon juice

¼ teaspoon black pepper

½ cup crumbled feta cheese

Bring a medium pot of salted water to a boil. Have ready a bowl of ice water. Add the peas to the boiling water and cook until they begin to float, 2 to 3 minutes. Sample a pea before draining: You want to cook them just until the vegetal flavor disappears, but the peas are still very green. Drain the peas and immediately transfer to the ice bath. Once cool, drain well.

In a mixing bowl, combine the peas with the mint, olive oil, lemon juice, 1 teaspoon salt, and the pepper. Transfer to a serving dish and top with the feta.

TURNIPS CAN BE a misunderstood vegetable, because when they are old or improperly cooked they are not that impressive. But pulled straight from the dirt when they are golf ball size or smaller, they taste like turnips should taste. I don't cook them for this recipe because they are perfectly tender and spicy as is. Cooking would take away their natural horseradish bite. A simple vinaigrette makes them a great side for any meat or fish dish, or for a lunch plate with buttered rye bread and sharp aged cheese.

MUSTARD-MARINATED
Turnips

SERVES 4 TO 6

2 bunches young turnip bulbs (about ½ pound), trimmed

3 tablespoons muscadine or red wine vinegar

2 tablespoons whole-grain mustard

2 tablespoons extra-virgin olive oil

½ cup thinly sliced scallions

½ cup chopped fresh flat-leaf parsley leaves

½ teaspoon kosher salt

¼ teaspoon black pepper

Cut the turnips in half or quarters to make varied bite-size pieces. Whisk together the remaining ingredients in a medium mixing bowl, then add the turnips, and toss to combine. Marinate in the fridge for an hour or up to 4 hours to allow the flavors to develop.

ONE OF THE most exciting ingredients I saw in the markets of France was the onion. Each one had its top attached and there wasn't a brown skin in sight. Cooking with these fresh spring onions changed the way I think about them: Instead of being simply an ingredient in stocks and sauces, the onion can be the star on its own. This dish stands alone as a side or can be used to top grilled ham, roast lamb, whole fish, or just about any savory dish.

SWEET AND SOUR
Spring Onions

SERVES 4 TO 6

6 spring onions, each 2½ inches wide
1 tablespoon olive oil
1 teaspoon kosher salt
¼ teaspoon black pepper, plus more to taste
1 cup red wine vinegar
3 tablespoons sugar
1 (3-inch) rosemary sprig
1 garlic clove, thinly sliced
Flaky sea salt

Preheat the oven to 450°F.

Rinse the onions well under running water, as the outer layers typically conceal dirt and grit. Leaving a portion of the stem end attached (so the onions will hold together), quarter the onions. Put the onions in a glass or ceramic baking dish, toss them with the olive oil, kosher salt, and ¼ teaspoon pepper, and roast until the onions are softened and beginning to caramelize on the bottom, about 15 minutes.

Meanwhile, in a medium bowl, whisk together the vinegar and sugar until the sugar has dissolved. Add the rosemary and garlic. Heat a cast-iron skillet over medium-high heat. Pour the vinegar mixture into the skillet and bring to a simmer. Reduce the heat and simmer until the mixture has reduced by three-quarters and thickened to the consistency of thin honey. Add the onions and stir gently to combine. Cook over low heat until the onions are glazed with the syrup, a few minutes.

To serve, transfer the onions and syrup to a plate and finish with a sprinkling of flaky sea salt and black pepper.

EGGPLANT IS EVERYWHERE in the South in the summer. I grew up eating it mostly fried, which is great, but I also like it simply grilled until the flesh is tender and smoky, and tossed with vinegar and mint. Serve this luscious side dish with fish or lamb.

MARINATED EGGPLANT
with Chile Flakes and Mint

SERVES 6 TO 8

2 large eggplants (1 to 1½ pounds total)

3 tablespoons extra-virgin olive oil

1 tablespoon kosher salt

1 teaspoon black pepper

3 tablespoons sherry wine vinegar

½ teaspoon red pepper flakes

1 cup looselwy packed fresh mint leaves, torn into ½-inch pieces

Heat your grill to medium-high.

Beginning at the stem end, use a vegetable peeler to peel vertical stripes down the eggplant, leaving half of the skin intact. Slice the eggplant into ½-inch-thick rounds.

Pour 1 tablespoon of the oil onto a rimmed baking sheet. Brush the eggplant rounds with the oil in the pan and season both sides with 2 teaspoons of the salt and the black pepper.

Grill until the eggplant is soft and no longer raw in the middle, about 5 minutes per side. Be careful not to overcook the eggplant or it will get very mushy. Use tongs to transfer to a plate. When the rounds are cool enough to handle, cut each one into 6 triangles.

In a medium bowl, combine the vinegar, the remaining 2 tablespoons oil, remaining 1 teaspoon salt, and the red pepper flakes. Add the eggplant and mint and gently toss to combine.

Marinate for about an hour at room temperature to allow flavors to develop.

To SALT OR NOT TO Salt

Traditional wisdom calls for you to salt eggplant before cooking to get it to release its excess moisture and any bitterness. I tried both methods for this recipe—salting and not salting. Salting the eggplant first made it darken quickly and dry out. The benefit is that it did not absorb as much oil in the cooking process. However, I find that presalting the eggplant detracts from its natural flavor, so I prefer not to do it.

I HAVE NOT met many people who know how to make couscous properly, so when I show them they are always amazed at how simple it is. The key to good couscous is salt and olive oil: You need plenty of each. I love preparing it as a side dish, because the flavors can be altered to complement the main course. I have yet to find a meat that doesn't work beautifully with couscous. The mint in this version ties in well with lamb in particular.

FRESH MINT
Couscous

SERVES 6 TO 8

2 cups couscous
½ cup finely minced onion
½ cup finely chopped carrot
1½ teaspoons kosher salt
½ teaspoon black pepper
¼ cup extra-virgin olive oil
½ cup mint leaves, thinly sliced

In a medium mixing bowl, combine the couscous, onion, carrot, salt, and pepper.

Bring 2 cups water to a boil and pour over the mixture. Stir quickly with a fork, cover tightly with plastic wrap, and let sit for 10 minutes.

Uncover and mix in the mint and olive oil with a fork, fluffing up the couscous and breaking up any lumps that may form. Serve warm or at room temperature.

TWO MAINSTAYS OF Cajun cooking, rice and pork, create the perfect picnic salad or an easy summer supper. Chopped onions and scallions, along with a handful of fresh tomatoes and herbs, add plenty of vibrant flavors. A few spoonfuls of Creole mustard and minced chile peppers give it plenty of zip.

This salad can be made a day in advance and refrigerated, but for the fullest flavor and the best texture, serve it at room temperature. Rice becomes hard and waxy when it's cold.

SMOKED HAM AND RICE
Salad

SERVES 6 TO 8

1 cup white rice

1 cup small-diced smoked ham

12 cherry tomatoes, halved or quartered

½ cup coarsely chopped fresh flat-leaf parsley

½ red onion, cut into small dice

¼ cup thinly sliced scallions

1 jalapeño, stemmed, seeded, and minced

3 tablespoons red wine vinegar, or more to taste

3 tablespoons extra-virgin olive oil

3 tablespoons Creole mustard

1 teaspoon kosher salt, or more to taste

¼ teaspoon black pepper, or more to taste

Combine the rice with 1½ cups water in a medium saucepan. Bring to a boil over medium-high heat, cover, and reduce the heat to low. Simmer for 18 minutes. Remove from the heat and let rest for 10 minutes, covered, to allow the rice to finish cooking. Fluff the rice with a fork.

In a large mixing bowl, combine the rice with the remaining ingredients, using a rubber spatula to mix well and making sure to break up any large clumps of rice. Taste for seasonings and add more salt, pepper, or vinegar as desired.

LOUISIANA WEATHER IN the winter can be all over the place. One particular year we had a long hot spell and the broccoli in our garden began to bolt and flower. I cut all the florets and yellow flowers (which are edible), leaving an inch or two of the stalk, and played with this Italian-style method of quick-cooking them. The high heat and oil really intensify the flavors in the broccoli. You may be tempted to add water to this, but don't. If you're not rescuing bolting broccoli, you can get a similar effect by slicing the broccoli really thin through the florets.

I-TALIAN STYLE
Broccoli

SERVES 4

1 tablespoon extra-virgin olive oil

1 head broccoli, florets thinly sliced (about 4 cups)

1 tablespoon thinly sliced garlic

½ teaspoon red pepper flakes

½ teaspoon kosher salt

1 lemon wedge

Heat a cast-iron skillet over high heat. Pour in the oil, swirl to coat, and then add the broccoli, garlic, red pepper flakes, and salt and cook until the broccoli turns bright green and the garlic just starts to brown, 4 to 5 minutes.

Squeeze the lemon over the broccoli and serve.

WHEN MY COUSINS in Louisiana get together, you can count on at least fifty people for dinner. At one particular gathering I attended, they had slaughtered one of their lambs, cut the meat into steaks, grilled them, and served them with this macaroni salad. I thought it was a genius way to create a side dish that could be so delicious and feed so many people. This macaroni has all the makings and style of a traditional potato salad, but the pasta makes it lighter and brighter, perfect for an untraditional barbecue.

CAJUN MACARONI
Salad

SERVES 8 TO 10

Kosher salt

1 pound elbow macaroni

1 tablespoon extra-virgin olive oil

½ yellow onion, minced

4 celery stalks, cut into small dice

2 teaspoons paprika

1 teaspoon cayenne

1 teaspoon black pepper

3 tablespoons Creole mustard

1½ cups mayonnaise

3 tablespoons red wine vinegar

Juice of 1 lemon

1 teaspoon hot sauce, such as Louisiana or Tabasco, or more to taste

Bring a large pot of salted water to a boil, add the macaroni, and cook according to package directions. Drain, rinse with cold water, and drain again. Transfer to a large bowl and toss the noodles with the olive oil.

Use a rubber spatula to combine the remaining ingredients plus ½ cup water and 4 teaspoons salt. Taste for seasonings and adjust the salt and hot sauce as needed. Add the noodles and toss to combine. Add more water if needed to give the mixture a smooth, creamy appearance (or if it's going to sit in the refrigerator for more than 30 minutes before serving).

CAULIFLOWER IS AN underrated and underappreciated vegetable. When eaten plain or raw it really is not very exciting. However, when combined with cream, curry, or cheese—or best of all, all of them—it transforms into a sleeper hit. When serving this dish, remember that it is very rich and intense and only a small portion is needed: It works great as a side but can also be used in place of a sauce for almost any meat dish.

CAULIFLOWER
and
GRUYÈRE
Gratin

SERVES 8 TO 12

4 tablespoons (½ stick) unsalted butter, plus more for the dish

½ large onion, thinly sliced

1 tablespoon curry powder, preferably homemade (see page 186)

2 teaspoons kosher salt

1 teaspoon white pepper

1 teaspoon garam masala

3 tablespoons all-purpose flour

3 cups whole milk

2 cups heavy cream

1 tablespoon chopped fresh thyme

1 large head cauliflower or 3 small heads, cut into 1½-inch pieces (about 12 cups)

1 tablespoon plus 1 teaspoon fresh lemon juice

2 cups grated Gruyère cheese

1½ cups panko (Japanese bread crumbs)

Preheat the oven to 375°F. Butter a 9 × 13-inch baking dish.

Melt 2 tablespoons of the butter in a large saucepan. Add the onion and cook slowly over low heat until soft and translucent, 5 to 7 minutes. Add the curry powder, salt, pepper, and garam masala. Cook, stirring to combine and heat the spices, for 3 minutes. Add the flour and cook, stirring, until the ingredients are well combined.

Slowly pour in the milk and cream, stirring well to fully incorporate. Add the thyme and simmer for 5 minutes. Add the cauliflower and lemon juice. Cover and cook for about 5 minutes.

Add the cheese, stir to incorporate, and pour into the prepared baking dish. Melt the remaining 2 tablespoons butter and combine with the bread crumbs. Top the cauliflower with the bread crumbs and bake until the cauliflower is tender and the bread crumbs are golden brown, about 30 minutes. Let rest for 5 to 10 minutes before serving.

I LOVE THE new direction of Southern food using more worldly ingredients and different preparations, but this is one dish that I just wouldn't touch. Every time I eat this I am transported back to my grandad's kitchen and the warmth and security of what it feels like when the smells of ham hocks and fresh shelled peas are hanging in the air and everything in the world is perfect.

HAM HOCKS *and* CROWDER PEAS

SERVES 6 TO 8

2 smoked ham hocks

1 onion, cut into medium dice

2 bay leaves

2 pounds shelled fresh crowder peas or other field peas

1 tablespoon plus 1 teaspoon kosher salt

1 teaspoon black pepper

3 tablespoons Easy Pickled Chile Vinegar (page 168)

To make the broth, combine the hocks, onion, bay leaves, and 3½ quarts water in a medium heavy-bottomed pot. Bring to a boil over high heat and then reduce the heat so that the water simmers. Cover and cook until the ham hocks are completely tender, about 4 hours.

Add the peas, salt, and pepper and cook until the peas are tender, 30 to 45 minutes. Make sure the peas have enough liquid to cover them throughout the cooking process. If the liquid seems to be evaporating too quickly, cover the pot. The liquid should soak up into the beans as they cook; when they are done, the liquid level should be even with the peas.

Stir in the chile vinegar before serving.

WHITE BEANS ARE the most versatile of all beans because they take on the flavor of whatever they are cooked with—in this case tasso, cured seasoned pork shoulder (you can use diced slab bacon as a substitute). This casserole is great for potluck dinners because you can make it ahead of time and reheat it when you're ready to serve.

TASSO *and* WHITE BEAN *Gratin*

SERVES 8 TO 10

3 cups dried white beans

¼ pound tasso, diced

1 tablespoon unsalted butter

1 onion, diced

1 carrot, diced

4 celery stalks, diced

1 tablespoon minced garlic

1 tablespoon chopped fresh thyme

2 bay leaves

6 cups chicken broth

1 teaspoon kosher salt

½ teaspoon black pepper

1 cup panko (Japanese bread crumbs)

¼ cup chopped fresh flat-leaf parsley leaves

½ cup grated Parmesan cheese

3 tablespoons extra-virgin olive oil

Soak the beans overnight in enough water to cover them by at least 3 inches. Rinse and drain well.

In a large skillet, render the tasso in the butter over medium-high heat until just crispy. Add the onion, carrot, celery, and garlic and cook, stirring, until they start to soften, about 6 minutes. Add the thyme, bay leaves, chicken broth, and white beans and bring to a boil. Reduce the heat so the broth simmers gently. Cook the beans until they are completely tender, 35 to 45 minutes. This time will vary with the age of the dried beans. Season with ½ teaspoon of the salt and ¼ teaspoon of the pepper.

While the beans finish cooking, heat the oven to 450°F.

Meanwhile, mix the panko with the parsley, cheese, olive oil, and the remaining ½ teaspoon salt and ¼ teaspoon pepper. Pour the cooked beans into a 9 × 13-inch baking dish. Sprinkle the bread crumbs over the beans and bake until the crumbs are golden brown, about 15 minutes.

MY EARLY TRAINING days were heavily rooted in French cooking and technique, and this is one dish that has stuck with me for the long haul. It is essentially a potato dauphinoise using sweet potatoes, which are everywhere in the South. Normally I wouldn't mess with such a great classic, but the sweet potatoes impart another layer of richness and a touch of sweetness that elevate the whole.

SWEET POTATO
Gratin

SERVES 8 TO 10

Unsalted butter, for the baking dish

3 medium Yukon gold potatoes (about 1¼ pounds), thinly sliced

1 large sweet potato (about 1¼ pounds), peeled, cut in half lengthwise, and thinly sliced
2 tablespoons kosher salt

4 teaspoons black pepper

2 tablespoons chopped fresh thyme

2 cups grated Gruyère cheese

1 medium onion, thinly sliced

3 cups heavy cream

Heat the oven to 325°F.

Butter a 9 × 13-inch baking dish. Alternate layers of white and sweet potatoes, starting with the Yukon gold, and sprinkle each layer with salt and pepper, thyme, Gruyère, and onion. Press down on each layer and pour in enough of the cream to just cover. Repeat until all of the ingredients are used.

Bake until the potatoes are completely tender when pierced with a knife and the cheese is bubbly and browned, about 2 hours and 15 minutes.

Allow the gratin to cool for 30 minutes to 1 hour before serving.

Southern-Style SWEETS

Sea Salt Turtles 210

GRAPEFRUIT AND MINT
GRANITA 211

Cream Soda Sherbet 213

SALTED CARAMEL PEANUT
BRITTLE ICE CREAM 214

Zucker Platschen
(German Sugar Cookies) 216

HOLIDAY SHORTBREAD WITH
LEMON ICING 219

Triple-Chip Chocolate Chubbies 222

WHITE CHOCOLATE
MACADAMIA BLONDIES 223

McGaws' Extra-Bittersweet Chocolate
Chunk Monster Cookies 225

HEATH BAR BROWNIES WITH
FUDGY CHOCOLATE ICING 226

Orange Cream Cheese Bars with
Shortbread Crust 229

SPICED APPLE PECAN
BREAD 230

Zucchini Walnut Bread 232

BING CHERRY AND WHITE
CHOCOLATE BREAD
PUDDING 233

Banana Pudding with Moonshine
Whipped Cream 235

CHOCOLATE PEANUT BUTTER
PIE WITH CANDIED SPICY
PEANUTS 237

Aunt Sally's Coconut Pie 240

MISSISSIPPI MUD PIE WITH
CHOCOLATE GRAHAM CRACKER
CRUST AND CHOCOLATE ICE
CREAM 242

Roasted Fig Brown Butter Tart 245

LEMON BLACKBERRY TARTLET
WITH SWEET MASCARPONE 246

A Southern meal that ends without a little something sweet is like an unfinished sentence. It's like boudin without cold beer, or a holiday meal without gravy.

The South's passion for desserts is well established, but our fondness for sweets is not just about sugar. The appearance of a meringue-topped pie, a tin of homemade chocolate candies, or a platter of cookies extends the good times. Desserts draw out a family reunion, a dinner party, or a backyard barbecue. They encourage a second cup of coffee (or nip of single-barrel bourbon), another log on the fire. More often than not, we're not quite ready to end the chitchat or late-night boozy conversations, and homemade desserts give us a delicious reason to linger longer around the table.

There's also an argument that desserts, more than any other food, are a Southerner's ultimate expression of caring and affection. The aunt who drops by with a tin of cookies; a grandma who makes your favorite pie each time you visit; parents rolling out holiday shortbread cookies every December (and the flurry of icing that ensues); some of our favorite customers who bring warm chocolate chip cookies into the restaurant for the staff (no kidding)—these are gestures of kindness that you just can't buy. In our increasingly fast-paced, digital world, a birthday cake made from scratch or a pie baked for a loved one is a link to our culinary past, and keeps us grounded in traditions and rituals that give our lives more meaning.

Desserts are also sublime showcases for some of the South's best ingredients. Peanuts are made for brittle; pecans are classic for buttery cookies and rich, gooey bars; citrus fruits shine in brightly flavored granitas and creamy curds. Fruits like figs and blackberries star in sophisticated tarts. I never tire of iconic sweets like banana pudding, bread pudding, and coconut pies—but I have to say they're even more appealing when given an update, like a pinch of sea salt or a splash of a small-batch spirit.

You'll find plenty in this chapter to satisfy your sweet tooth and keep your loved ones around the table longer.

CHOCOLATE, NUTS, AND caramel are one of the world's great flavor combinations. A finish of coarse sea salt gives these turtles a grown-up edge.

SEA SALT
Turtles

MAKES 2 DOZEN

½ cup pecan halves

½ cup peanuts, plus some finely chopped for garnish

½ cup cashews

1 cup sugar

1 vanilla bean, split and scraped

⅔ cup sweetened condensed milk

½ cup light corn syrup

6 tablespoons (¾ stick) unsalted butter

½ teaspoon coarse sea salt, plus more for garnish

1 pound dark chocolate chips

Heat the oven to 350°F.

Combine the pecans, peanuts, and cashews on a rimmed baking sheet in a single layer and bake until lightly toasted, about 10 minutes.

Line another baking sheet with parchment paper. Arrange the toasted nuts on the lined pan in small clusters to resemble a turtle with the "legs" and "head" sticking out. You should have about 2 dozen clusters.

Prepare an ice bath.

To make the caramel, heat the sugar, vanilla bean and seeds, sweetened condensed milk, corn syrup, butter, and ¼ cup water in a medium saucepan over medium-low heat, stirring constantly to avoid scorching the milk, until the mixture comes to a boil. Attach a candy thermometer to the pot and cook the caramel until it reaches 242°F. Remove from the heat and stir in the salt. Carefully remove the vanilla bean and scrape into the caramel any seeds that cling to the bean.

Carefully lower the bottom of the caramel saucepan into the ice water while stirring. Remove the pan after just a few seconds: You want to cool the sugar quickly, maintaining a thick yet fluid consistency (about 145°F). Scoop or spoon the caramel onto the nut clusters so that they'll hold together. Set aside to cool and firm up for at least 3 hours or overnight.

When you're ready to finish the turtles, melt the chocolate chips in a double boiler or a bowl set over a saucepan of simmering water. Coat each cluster with a drizzle of chocolate and then garnish with a sprinkling of finely chopped peanuts and a little sea salt.

IF YOU'RE PREPARING several different dishes for dinner or planning a particularly rich meal, it's nice to have something fresh, bright, and simple for dessert. Granita is the perfect solution, because it's a palate cleanser, and a fantastic way to enjoy the season's best fruit juices. And—major bonus—it can be prepared a day or two in advance.

There's an amazing citrus culture in and around New Orleans. One of my favorite sources is Isabelle's Organic Orchard, a farm on the banks of the Mississippi that produces the best Meyer lemons, navel oranges, and grapefruit that I've ever tasted. According to the farmer, Isabelle Cossart, the river washed the most fertile topsoil from the Midwest and piled it up on the riverbanks. The rich, unique composition of that dirt creates its own *terroir,* along with some spectacular-tasting fruit.

This granita is perfectly refreshing on its own, but it's also delicious served with sugar cookies like Zucker Platschen (page 216), or squares of bitter chocolate.

GRAPEFRUIT
and MINT
Granita

SERVES 6 TO 8

½ cup sugar

Grated zest of 1 large lemon

2½ cups fresh grapefruit juice

½ cup loosely packed fresh mint leaves, thinly sliced

Combine the sugar, lemon zest, and 1 cup water in a small saucepan. Bring the mixture to a boil, stirring to dissolve the sugar. Remove from the heat and let cool to room temperature.

Combine the cooled syrup, grapefruit juice, and mint in a 9-inch square glass or ceramic baking dish. Put the baking dish in the freezer until the syrup is completely frozen, 2 to 3 hours.

When you're ready to serve, scrape the granita with a spoon or fork to flake it into pieces. Scoop the granita into chilled or frozen cups and serve.

WHO DIDN'T LOVE orange sherbet as a kid—especially after a hot summer day of swimming and playing outside? Sherbet is the refreshing middle ground between sorbet, made of juice and sugar, and full-on ice cream. A small amount of heavy cream rounds out sherbet's refreshing, icy texture.

Cream soda gives this recipe a nostalgic flavor that takes me back to push-up pops from the ice cream truck and the root beer floats we made at home on the weekends. Barq's Red Cream Soda creates a wild pink color that will be a hit with both kids and grown-ups.

CREAM SODA
Sherbet

MAKES 2 QUARTS

1½ cups sugar
⅔ cup light corn syrup
1 vanilla bean, split and scraped
1 quart heavy cream
2 (12-ounce) cans of your favorite cream soda

If you're using a canister-style ice cream machine, freeze the canister for at least 12 hours or, preferably, for 24 hours.

Heat the sugar, corn syrup, vanilla bean, and half of the cream in a heavy 2-quart saucepan over medium heat, stirring, until the mixture comes to a boil. Remove from the heat and stir in the remaining cream. Refrigerate the mixture for at least an hour.

Remove the vanilla bean and discard. Stir in the cream soda and freeze according to the manufacturer's instructions, until the sherbet has the texture of soft-serve ice cream.

Serve immediately, or transfer to a storage container and freeze until needed.

BLAME IT ON the Salted Nut Rolls that I used to tuck into my jacket pockets for fishing trips—I am crazy about peanuts and caramel. In this recipe, a rich vanilla ice cream flavored with swirls of salty caramel and peanut butter is studded with crunchy bites of peanut brittle. It's a pretty over-the-top combination, and the perfect punctuation to a dinner party. An unexpected sting of cayenne helps balance the sweetness. When you're making the candy, note that peanut brittle demands a slow, steady stir. If your peanut brittle is pale or milky white and granular, it probably was either not heated to the proper temperature or was stirred too vigorously during cooking.

SALTED CARAMEL PEANUT BRITTLE
Ice Cream

MAKES 2 QUARTS

1 quart heavy cream
1¼ cups sugar
2 tablespoons light corn syrup
1 vanilla bean, split and scraped
1 cup whole milk
¼ teaspoon kosher salt
8 large egg yolks
½ cup smooth peanut butter
½ recipe Peanut Brittle (recipe follows)

If you're using a canister-style ice cream machine, freeze the ice cream machine canister for at least 12 hours or, preferably, for 24 hours.

Heat 1 cup of the heavy cream in a small, heavy saucepan over medium heat until it comes to a boil. Remove from the heat, cover the pan to keep warm, and set aside.

Prepare an ice bath.

Combine the sugar, corn syrup, and vanilla bean and seeds in a heavy-bottomed saucepan and slowly cook over medium heat, stirring constantly until all the sugar has dissolved. Stop stirring and continue to cook to a golden caramel. Remove from the heat. Carefully stir in the hot cream, stirring until fully blended.

Add the milk and salt and return the pan to medium heat, stirring, until the mixture comes to a boil. Carefully remove the vanilla bean and scrape into the caramel any seeds that cling to the bean. Return the mixture to a simmer.

Put the yolks in a medium bowl and whisk them lightly. Temper the yolks by gradually adding about one-third of the hot milk mixture, whisking constantly. Return the egg mixture to the milk mixture in the saucepan and cook, stirring constantly with a wooden spoon over medium heat, until the custard base thickens enough to coat the back of the spoon.

Strain the custard base through a fine sieve into a storage container (a bowl shape is best since you'll be whisking) and transfer to the ice bath. Add the peanut butter and whisk to incorporate completely.

Stir in the remaining 3 cups heavy cream. Cover and refrigerate for at least 12 hours.

Freeze in an ice cream machine according to the manufacturer's instructions, until the mixture has the consistency of soft-serve ice cream. Fold in the broken peanut brittle pieces (if your ice cream maker has an opening, add the crushed brittle toward the end of the mixing time, once the ice cream has thickened). Transfer the ice cream to a storage container and freeze for several hours or overnight to allow the flavors to meld before serving.

Peanut Brittle

MAKES ABOUT 3 CUPS

1¾ cups sugar

1¼ cups light corn syrup

12 ounces salted roasted peanuts, chopped

1½ teaspoons kosher salt

Pinch of cayenne

2 tablespoons unsalted butter

1 teaspoon vanilla extract

1 teaspoon baking soda

Combine the sugar, corn syrup, and ½ cup plus 2 tablespoons water in a heavy-bottomed saucepan over high heat. Stir constantly to ensure that the sugar is moistened, so it will dissolve evenly and not scorch. When the syrup comes to a boil, stop stirring. Continue to cook to the hardball stage, 264°F on a candy thermometer.

Stir in the peanuts, salt, and cayenne. Continue cooking, stirring slowly and gently with a wooden spoon, until the mixture reaches the hard crack stage, 318°F on a candy thermometer. As a general rule, if the mixture has reached the proper temperature but the color is not fully developed, continue cooking until the mixture has a golden-brown caramel color.

Remove from the heat carefully and stir in the butter and vanilla until incorporated. Stir in the baking soda.

Pour the mixture onto a lightly oiled marble work surface or a baking sheet lined with a silicone mat. Allow the brittle to cool slightly until it has a pliable plastic texture. Wearing latex gloves to protect your hands, pull the brittle out from the edges and break it into pieces as it hardens. This must be done quickly, before the brittle hardens completely. The pieces will be all different shapes and sizes.

Allow the brittle to cool completely and then break it into smaller, bite-size pieces. Store in a completely dry, airtight container for up to 2 weeks.

MY GERMAN GRANDPARENTS, aunts, and uncles provided me with a steady fix of these cookies throughout my childhood; as such they remain a weakness of mine. To me this is the perfect version of a sugar cookie—thin and crisp, with a deep, pure butter flavor. These are traditionally cut into circles, but feel free to follow your whim and cut them into any shape you wish.

ZUCKER PLATSCHEN
(German Sugar Cookies)

MAKES ABOUT 3 DOZEN COOKIES

4 tablespoons (½ stick) unsalted butter, at room temperature

1 cup plus 2 tablespoons sugar

1 large egg

2 tablespoons whole milk

½ teaspoon vanilla extract

2 cups all-purpose flour, plus more for rolling

1½ teaspoons baking powder

Colored sugar or Cinnamon Sugar (page 231), for garnish

In an electric mixer fitted with the paddle attachment, beat the butter and sugar on medium-high speed until light and creamy, 2 to 3 minutes. Stir in the egg, milk, and vanilla.

In a separate bowl, whisk together the flour and baking powder. Gradually stir them into the butter mixture.

Divide the dough in half, wrap each half in plastic, and refrigerate for at least 20 minutes, or up to 3 days.

Heat the oven to 350°F. Line 2 baking sheets with parchment paper.

Working with half the dough at a time, roll the dough out very thin (about ¼ inch) on a lightly floured surface (flouring your rolling pin as needed). Use a cookie cutter to make 3-inch circles (or your desired shape), and use an offset metal spatula to carefully transfer the cookies to the prepared baking sheet. Sprinkle the cookies with colored sugar and bake until the edges are a light golden brown, about 10 minutes.

Transfer the cookies to a wire rack to cool completely. To retain a crisp texture, store in an airtight container for up to 2 weeks.

AMANDA AND THE kids look forward to making this delicious shortbread every year. You use your fingers to press the dough into a tart pan, and who doesn't like to play with buttery dough? The addition of sliced almonds, toasted in the oven, and lemony icing makes these rich triangles of shortbread a pleasure to gobble up with a cup of espresso, or—my kids' favorite—a big glass of cold milk.

HOLIDAY SHORTBREAD
with
Lemon Icing

MAKES 12 WEDGES

16 tablespoons (2 sticks) unsalted butter, cold, cut into cubes

¼ teaspoon kosher salt

¼ cup confectioners' sugar

¼ cup granulated sugar, plus more for garnish

2 cups pastry flour, plus more for shaping

½ cup sliced almonds

Lemon Icing (recipe follows)

Preheat the oven to 350°F.

In the bowl of an electric mixer fitted with the paddle attachment, beat the butter and salt on low speed until softened, 2 to 3 minutes. Add the confectioners' sugar and granulated sugar, increase the mixer speed to medium, and beat, scraping down the sides of the bowl as needed, until light and fluffy, 3 to 4 minutes. Add the flour in 3 batches, turning the mixer off before each addition and mixing on low until just combined.

Turn the dough out onto a lightly floured work surface, gather into a ball, and flatten into a disc. Using your hands, press the dough into a 9½-inch tart pan with a removable base. Sprinkle the top of the dough with extra sugar and the sliced almonds.

Bake for 15 minutes, then decrease the oven temperature to 300°F, and bake until light golden, an additional 25 minutes.

Remove the pan from the oven. Press up on the bottom of the tart pan to release the sides of the pan. Using a long knife, slice the shortbread into 12 even wedges while still warm. Allow the wedges to cool completely.

Drizzle the icing over the cookies using a fork. Let set before transferring to an airtight tin.

Lemon Icing

MAKES ABOUT 1 CUP

1¼ cups confectioners' sugar
2 tablespoons fresh lemon
 juice
½ teaspoon vanilla extract

Whisk together the confectioners' sugar, lemon juice, and vanilla in a small bowl.

VARIATION

Shortbread Cookies

These cookies also make great holiday cutouts—simply turn the dough out onto a lightly floured work surface, roll it to your desired thickness (using extra flour as needed), and cut into shapes with your favorite cutters. Chill the cutouts in the freezer on the baking sheet for an hour before baking. Sprinkle with vanilla sugar or colored holiday sugars and bake until light golden, about 12 minutes. Transfer the cookies to a wire rack to cool completely. Reroll scraps until all of the dough is used. Store the cookies in an airtight tin for up to 2 weeks.

I HAVE ALWAYS been a chocolate fanatic. I'm one of those people who actually gets a mellowing buzz of tranquility from chocolate. But I don't like watered-down versions of sweet chocolate: I like the full-on, intense power of quality chocolate. One of my favorite guilty pleasures is indulging in these chocolate cookies with my morning coffee.

TRIPLE-CHIP
Chocolate Chubbies

MAKES 2½ DOZEN COOKIES

⅓ cup all-purpose flour

¼ teaspoon baking powder

⅛ teaspoon kosher salt

2½ cups bittersweet chocolate chips

4 ounces unsweetened baking chocolate, coarsely chopped

8 tablespoons (1 stick) unsalted butter

4 large eggs

1¾ cups sugar

1 cup milk chocolate chips

1 cup white chocolate chips

Sift the flour, baking powder, and salt into a bowl.

Melt 1½ cups of the bittersweet chips, the unsweetened chocolate, and butter together in a double boiler or a bowl set over a pan of gently simmering water. Remove from the heat.

In the bowl of an electric mixer fitted with the paddle attachment, beat the eggs and sugar on medium speed until light and fluffy, about 5 minutes. Decrease the speed and add the melted chocolate mixture. Mix well, scraping the sides and bottom of the bowl as needed with a rubber spatula.

Continue to mix on low speed and add the flour mixture. Mix, scraping the bowl, until all the flour is incorporated. Stir in the remaining 1 cup bittersweet chips along with the milk and white chocolate chips until just combined. Refrigerate the batter for at least 20 minutes.

When you're ready to bake, heat the oven to 350°F. Line 2 baking sheets with parchment paper.

Using a ¼-cup measure (or a small ice cream scoop), scoop the dough, roll it into balls, and arrange about 1½ inches apart on the prepared baking sheets. Bake, rotating the sheets halfway through baking, until the cookies are set and slightly puffed and cracked in the center, 13 to 15 minutes. Allow the cookies to cool briefly on the baking sheets before transferring them to a wire rack to cool completely.

Store in an airtight tin for up to 1 week.

OKAY, SO WHITE chocolate and macadamia nuts aren't the most Southern ingredients, but they are impossibly delicious together. These bars have become a favorite of mine, and this is a recipe that I've relied on for countless parties (for both kids and adults).

White chocolate gets a bad rap, because it's not "real chocolate" or the choice for purists. But I think it's underrated, and it works beautifully as a sweet backdrop for other ingredients. In these blondies, for instance, the white chocolate chips disappear into the mix and create a chewy texture and a toffee-like flavor with the buttery macadamia nuts. For the best texture, don't overbake these bars.

WHITE CHOCOLATE
Macadamia Blondies

MAKES 12 LARGE BARS

16 tablespoons (2 sticks) unsalted butter, at room temperature, plus more for the pan

2 cups all-purpose flour

1 teaspoon kosher salt

½ teaspoon baking soda

2½ cups packed dark brown sugar

4 large eggs

1 teaspoon vanilla extract

1 cup salted and roasted macadamia nuts, chopped

1 cup white chocolate chips

Heat the oven to 350°F. Butter a 9 × 13-inch baking dish.

Heat the butter in a small, heavy saucepan over medium heat until it foams up and then subsides. The butter should have a nutty aroma and a deep golden brown color. Remove from the heat and set on a cool surface to help stop the cooking.

Whisk together the flour, salt, and baking soda in a mixing bowl.

In a separate bowl, stir together the browned butter and the sugar. Whisk in the eggs and vanilla extract. Add the flour and fold in using a rubber spatula until just combined. Stir in the nuts and white chocolate chips.

Using a rubber spatula, spread the mixture into the prepared baking dish. Bake until a tester inserted in the center of the dough comes out clean, 45 to 55 minutes.

Allow to cool completely on a wire rack before slicing into 12 equal bars. Store in an airtight tin for up to 1 week.

EVERY SATURDAY THE entire staff at Herbsaint awaits the arrival of two of our favorite customers and friends, Wayne and Janis McGaw, who bring a warm tray of the most delicious cookies for every employee in the restaurant. When I first heard that they had invited the entire staff to their house for dinner and swimming, my reaction was, "Do they know what they're getting into?" The McGaws share an almost shocking level of hospitality, and they're an inspiration to us all.

The McGaws, and these hefty, chewy chocolate chip cookies that Wayne bakes with skill and love, are just two of the reasons I love New Orleans so much.

McGAWS' EXTRA-BITTERSWEET
Chocolate Chunk Monster Cookies

MAKES 8 GIANT COOKIES

8 tablespoons (1 stick) unsalted butter

¾ teaspoon vanilla extract

⅓ cup sugar

½ teaspoon kosher salt

1 cup all-purpose flour, sifted

1 cup chopped walnuts

9 ounces extra-bittersweet chocolate, chopped into 1-inch chunks

Heat the oven to 350°F. Line a baking sheet with parchment paper or aluminum foil, shiny-side up.

In the bowl of an electric mixer fitted with the paddle attachment, beat the butter until just barely soft. Beat in the vanilla, sugar, and salt and then mix in the flour until just incorporated. Using a heavy wooden spatula, stir in the nuts and chocolate.

Use a ⅓-cup measuring cup to scoop an even amount for each cookie. Roll each scoop of dough into a ball. Put the cookies on the prepared sheet and flatten to about ½ inch thick and 3½ inches wide.

Bake, rotating the sheet halfway through, until the cookies are a pale golden color and darker around the edges, 16 to 18 minutes. Allow the cookies to cool—at least slightly—before devouring.

WHEN I WAS a kid and old enough to have spare change in my pockets, I fell in love with Heath bars. I've retained a soft spot for chocolate plus toffee, so I couldn't resist making a brownie recipe a bit richer with the addition of both.

The chocolate icing isn't essential, but it definitely takes these moist, fudgy bars to the next level and creates a sublime experience for chocolate lovers.

HEATH BAR BROWNIES
with Fudgy Chocolate Icing

MAKES 12 LARGE BROWNIES

4 tablespoons (½ stick) unsalted butter, melted, plus more for the pan

⅓ cup Dutch-processed cocoa powder

2 ounces unsweetened chocolate, coarsely chopped

2¼ cups sugar

½ cup plus 2 tablespoons vegetable oil

2 large eggs

2 large egg yolks

1 teaspoon vanilla extract

1¾ cups all-purpose flour

1 teaspoon kosher salt

2 (8-ounce) packages Heath toffee bits (about 3 cups)

1 cup semisweet chocolate chips

Fudgy Chocolate Icing (recipe follows)

Heat the oven to 350°F. Butter a 9 × 13-inch baking dish.

In a bowl, whisk the cocoa powder with ½ cup plus 2 tablespoons boiling water.

Melt the chocolate and butter in a double boiler or a bowl set over a saucepan of simmering water. Whisk in the cocoa mixture.

In a large bowl, whisk together the sugar, oil, eggs, egg yolks, and vanilla. Whisk in the chocolate mixture. Sift the flour and salt into the batter, and stir to combine. Stir in 2½ cups of the toffee chips and the chocolate chips.

Use a rubber spatula to transfer the batter to the prepared baking dish. Bake until a tester inserted in the middle of the pan comes out clean, about 40 minutes. Allow the brownies to cool completely on a wire rack before icing.

Use a frosting knife to evenly ice the brownies and then sprinkle the remaining ½ cup toffee chips over the top. When you're ready to serve, slice the brownies into 12 equal bars. The brownies will keep in an airtight container for up to 1 week.

Fudgy Chocolate Icing

MAKES ABOUT 2 CUPS

6 tablespoons (¾ stick)
unsalted butter

1½ ounces unsweetened
chocolate, coarsely chopped

1 ounce bittersweet chocolate,
coarsely chopped

¼ cup sour cream

½ cup plus ⅓ cup
confectioners' sugar

Melt the butter and chocolate
in a double boiler or in a metal
bowl set over a pan of gently
simmering water.

Combine the sour cream and
sugar in a mixing bowl. Add the
warm, melted chocolate and
whisk until all ingredients are
combined and the icing is thick
and glossy. Set the icing aside
in a cool space to rest at least
for 1 hour, until it becomes
thick and spreadable.

THESE TART-SWEET BARS deliver a sunny citrus flavor, a rich, cheesecake-like texture, and a buttery shortbread crust. Because they're best made in advance and served chilled, they're great bar cookies to take to a potluck or a kids' party. I call for orange juice, but feel free to use the juice of satsumas or Meyer lemons when they're in season. These bars don't need a garnish, but if you're feeling fancy you can dust them with confectioners' sugar or serve them alongside citrus segments that have been tossed with a splash of Cointreau or Grand Marnier.

ORANGE CREAM CHEESE BARS
with Shortbread Crust

MAKES 12 LARGE BARS

CRUST

2 cups shortbread cookie crumbs, from homemade cookies (see page 219) or store-bought

¾ cup graham cracker crumbs

2 tablespoons sugar

8 tablespoons (1 stick) unsalted butter, melted

FILLING

1 cup fresh orange juice

1¼ cups sugar

1½ pounds cream cheese, at room temperature

1 tablespoon grated orange zest

¼ teaspoon kosher salt

4 large eggs

2 teaspoons vanilla extract

3 tablespoons fresh lemon juice

2 tablespoons orange juice concentrate

½ cup heavy cream

Heat the oven to 350°F. Line a 9 × 13-inch baking dish with parchment paper.

Make the crust: Combine the shortbread crumbs, graham cracker crumbs, sugar, and melted butter in a mixing bowl. Press the mixture into the bottom of the dish. Bake until light golden, about 10 minutes; set aside to cool.

Decrease the oven temperature to 300°F.

Meanwhile, prepare the filling: In a small, heavy saucepan, simmer the orange juice with ¼ cup of the sugar over medium heat, stirring, until you have ¼ cup liquid; set aside to cool.

In the bowl of an electric mixer fitted with the paddle attachment, beat the cream cheese with the remaining 1 cup sugar, the salt, and zest on medium-high until the cream cheese is completely soft and the sugar is fully incorporated, about 5 minutes. Make sure to scrape the bowl well. Reduce the speed to low and add the eggs one at a time, beating well after each addition. Add the vanilla and scrape down the bowl. Add the orange reduction, lemon juice, orange juice concentrate, and heavy cream and beat until blended.

Pour the batter into the cooled shortbread crust and bake until completely set, 40 minutes. Cool at room temperature for at least 2 hours and refrigerate for at least another 2 hours or overnight before serving.

Slice into 12 even squares and serve chilled.

THIS MOIST, AROMATIC bread should be your go-to recipe when the farmer's market is brimming with local apples. It's great to have around for breakfast, particularly when you have houseguests. The bread actually has the best flavor and texture if it's made the night before, so you'll look like a pro when you're slicing up homemade breakfast as the coffee is brewing. The bread is delicious as is, but it's also tasty broiled and buttered or slathered with cream cheese.

Note that you grate the apples with their skins on—this really enhances the apple flavor. Organic Granny Smith, Fuji, or Pink Lady apples are my favorite varieties to use, although any tart, crisp apple will work.

SPICED APPLE
Pecan Bread

MAKES ONE 9 × 5-INCH LOAF

2 tablespoons unsalted butter, plus more for the pan

1 cup plus 2 tablespoons all-purpose flour, plus more for the pan

½ cup pecans

3 medium apples

2 teaspoons fresh lemon juice

2 large eggs

1 teaspoon vanilla extract

¼ cup plus 1 tablespoon granulated sugar

¼ cup plus 2 tablespoons packed light brown sugar

⅓ cup vegetable oil

¼ teaspoon ground cinnamon

¾ teaspoon ground nutmeg

⅛ teaspoon ground ginger

½ teaspoon baking soda

1 teaspoon baking powder

¼ teaspoon kosher salt

2 tablespoons Cinnamon Sugar (recipe follows)

Heat the oven to 350°F.

Grease a loaf pan with melted butter and sprinkle with all-purpose flour. Turn the pan upside down and tap out the excess flour.

Put the pecans on a rimmed baking sheet and bake until fragrant and lightly browned, 7 to 9 minutes. Set aside to cool and then finely chop.

Core, peel, and dice one of the apples into ¼-inch cubes (you should have about 1 cup). Melt the 2 tablespoons butter in a medium skillet over medium-high heat and sauté the apple cubes, stirring, until soft and caramelized, about 7 minutes. Use a slotted spoon to transfer the apple to a plate lined with paper towels to cool and drain the apple excess moisture.

Core the remaining 2 apples and use a box grater to shred them onto paper towels (you'll have about 1½ cups). Use your hands to squeeze excess juice into a bowl (then you can drink the juice). The apples should be somewhat drier yet still moist. In a large bowl, toss together the shredded and diced apples, the pecans, lemon juice, and 2 tablespoons of the flour.

In a separate large bowl, whisk together the eggs, vanilla, granulated and brown sugars, and oil, making sure all the ingredients are completely incorporated.

In a third bowl, mix together the remaining 1 cup flour, the cinnamon, nutmeg, ginger, baking soda, baking powder, and salt. Use a spatula to fold the dry ingredients into the egg mixture. Stir in the apple and nut mixture. Transfer the batter to the prepared pan and sprinkle with cinnamon sugar.

Bake until a skewer inserted into the middle of the loaf comes out clean, about 50 minutes. Cool the bread in the pan for 5 minutes. Invert the bread onto a wire rack, turn right-side up, and let cool completely.

To store this bread, wrap it snugly in plastic wrap; it will keep for up to 3 days at room temperature.

Cinnamon Sugar

MAKES ¼ CUP

2 tablespoons granulated sugar

2 tablespoons raw sugar (such as turbinado)

½ teaspoon ground cinnamon

Combine all of the ingredients in a small bowl.

THIS RECIPE IS a classic end-of-summer outlet for garden zucchini. Kids love quick breads, and this one is a delicious and appealing way to get them to eat more vegetables.

Rosemary needles are very woody, so it's important to chop the rosemary very fine. I like to use my spice grinder for this task, because it will pulverize the needles and grind them almost to a powder.

ZUCCHINI WALNUT
Bread

MAKES ONE 9 × 5-INCH LOAF

Butter or nonstick cooking spray, for the pan

1½ cups plus 2 tablespoons all-purpose flour, plus more for the pan

½ cup walnuts

2 medium zucchini

1 teaspoon baking powder

1 teaspoon baking soda

¾ teaspoon kosher salt

1 teaspoon finely chopped fresh rosemary

1½ cups sugar

½ cup canola or olive oil

2 large eggs

Grated zest of 1 small lemon

1 teaspoon fresh lemon juice

Heat the oven to 350°F.

Grease a loaf pan with butter or cooking spray and dust the pan with flour. Turn the pan upside down and tap out the excess flour.

Spread the walnuts on a baking sheet and lightly toast in the oven until fragrant, 7 to 9 minutes. Set aside to cool and then coarsely chop. Using a box grater or a food processor fitted with a shredding disk, grate the zucchini. Measure out 2 cups. Spread the zucchini out on paper towels to absorb excess water.

Sift the flour, baking powder, baking soda, and salt into a bowl. Stir in the rosemary. In another bowl, whisk together the sugar, oil, and eggs. Use a spatula to fold the dry ingredients into the wet ingredients and then fold in the lemon zest, lemon juice, zucchini, and walnuts. Pour the batter into the prepared pan. Bake until a skewer inserted into the middle of the loaf comes out clean, about 50 minutes. Cool the bread in the pan for 5 minutes. Invert the bread onto a wire rack, turn right-side up, and let cool completely.

To store this bread, wrap it snugly in plastic wrap; it will keep for up to 3 days at room temperature.

WHEN MY KIDS were six and one, my wife, Amanda, and I decided we would spend some time in France. Paris can be a little challenging with two little ones, but the countryside in Burgundy was a dream for our family, and the region showed me what the real France is all about. As luck would have it, I happened to be in Chablis at my first French farmer's market on Father's Day. I couldn't believe the quality of the produce: It was the most remarkable thing I had ever seen—and I'd lived in San Francisco for six years. I went crazy buying enough fruits and vegetables to feed a town. The cherries were exceptionally gorgeous, so I bought tons. The next day I invited the couple who had rented us the house over for dinner, and spent all day prepping a five-course meal that ended with this white chocolate cherry bread pudding. I've seen recipes with dried cherries before, but after savoring this dish I could never make it with anything but the sweetest, juiciest summer cherries at their peak of ripeness—it's worth the wait.

BING CHERRY
and White Chocolate Bread Pudding

SERVES 12

8 cups 1-inch cubes day-old baguette

1½ cups sugar

8 large eggs

4 large egg yolks

1½ teaspoons vanilla extract

½ teaspoon kosher salt

1 quart heavy cream

Unsalted butter for the pan

2½ cups fresh Bing cherries (see Note), pitted and chopped

1 cup white chocolate chips

¼ cup Cinnamon Sugar (page 231)

Heat the oven to 325°F.

Put the bread cubes on a rimmed baking sheet and bake until lightly toasted, about 7 minutes. Set aside to cool completely.

Whisk together the sugar, eggs, yolks, vanilla, and salt in a large mixing bowl. Whisk in the cream. Add the bread cubes, stir to combine (pressing down on the bread so it will absorb the custard), and soak for 1 hour at room temperature (or up to 4 hours in the fridge).

Generously butter a 9 × 13-inch baking dish.

Stir the cherries and chocolate into the bread mixture, pour into the prepared baking dish, and sprinkle the cinnamon sugar over the top. Cover the dish with aluminum foil, put it on a baking sheet, and bake for 30 minutes. Uncover and continue baking until the custard is completely set and the top is lightly browned, about 20 minutes. Allow the pudding to cool for at least 20 minutes before serving.

NOTE: For the best results, use fresh seasonal cherries for this recipe. But if you crave this combination at other times, frozen organic cherries are an acceptable substitute. You'll want to add them when they're frozen to minimize how much they stain the rest of the batter pink.

BANANA PUDDING IS the creamy, soothing treat that Southern grandmas and aunts across the region prepare for their families. Creating individual parfaits makes for a pretty presentation, and it feels like a custom present when served after a dinner party. However, you can also layer these ingredients in an 8-inch square baking dish. Homemade vanilla wafers take this dessert to the next level.

We started serving Catdaddy Carolina Moonshine, a small-batch spirit made in North Carolina, at Cochon soon after it came out. Since then it's amassed a big following. The kick of the moonshine is a nice way to add some spice and character to whipped cream. So is bourbon.

BANANA PUDDING
with Moonshine Whipped Cream

SERVES 6

CUSTARD
1 tablespoon unflavored gelatin
2 cups heavy cream
1 vanilla bean, split and scraped
¾ cup sugar
Pinch of kosher salt
2 large eggs
10 large egg yolks
2 cups pureed ripe bananas (2 or 3 bananas)
1 tablespoon fresh lemon juice

3 ripe bananas, peeled and sliced
2 tablespoons plain yogurt
1 tablespoon fresh lemon juice
30 to 40 vanilla wafers, homemade (recipe follows) or store-bought
2 cups heavy cream
¼ cup sugar
¼ cup moonshine or bourbon

Make the custard: To bloom the gelatin, sprinkle it over the surface of ¼ cup cold water; set aside until the water has been absorbed, 5 to 10 minutes.

Combine the heavy cream, vanilla bean, half of the sugar, and the salt in a 2-quart saucepan over medium heat and cook, stirring, until the mixture comes to a simmer.

In a mixing bowl, whisk together the eggs, yolks, and remaining sugar. Temper the yolks by whisking in a third of the hot cream mixture. Whisk the tempered egg mixture into the remaining hot cream and continue to cook over medium heat, stirring with a wooden spoon, until the mixture thickens enough to coat the back of the spoon. Add the bloomed gelatin and mix well. Mix in the banana puree and lemon juice. Transfer the custard to a glass bowl, cover with plastic wrap pressed onto the surface, and refrigerate until set, at least 3 hours or overnight.

When you're ready to assemble the parfaits, toss the banana slices with the yogurt and lemon juice in a small bowl.

Crush the vanilla wafers slightly.

Whip the cream, sugar, and moonshine in an electric mixer on medium-high speed until stiff peaks form.

To assemble the parfaits, spread a small amount of the chilled pudding in the bottom of your dessert bowls or parfait glasses. Cover with a layer of broken vanilla wafers (you'll probably use 5 to 7 wafers for each parfait, depending on how much texture you want), followed

(recipe continues)

by a layer of banana slices. Spoon more of the pudding on top of the bananas and repeat, ending in a layer of pudding. Top the parfaits with a dollop of whipped cream and a whole vanilla wafer or two. Chill for at least 1 hour and up to 6 hours before serving.

Vanilla Wafers

MAKES ABOUT 60 SMALL COOKIES

8 tablespoons (1 stick) unsalted butter, at room temperature

1 cup sugar

¼ teaspoon kosher salt

1 vanilla bean, split and scraped

1 large egg

2 tablespoons whole milk

1½ teaspoons vanilla extract

1⅓ cups all-purpose flour

1 teaspoon baking powder

Heat the oven to 350°F. Line 2 baking sheets with parchment paper.

In the bowl of an electric mixer fitted with the paddle attachment, beat the butter, sugar, salt, and vanilla bean seeds on medium-high speed, until light and fluffy. Mix in the egg until well incorporated. Stir in the milk and vanilla. On low speed, add the flour and baking powder and mix until just blended. Scrape the mixing bowl to make sure everything has been incorporated.

Using a pastry bag, pipe the batter onto the baking sheets, making quarter-sized mounds about 1 inch apart. Bake, rotating the sheets halfway through baking, until the cookies are lightly browned on the edges, about 10 minutes. Remove from the oven and cool completely on wire racks. Store in an airtight container for up to 2 weeks.

EVERY YEAR MY sister makes this ethereal pie for the holidays—thanks, Michelle! Over the years I've discovered that not everyone likes the combination of chocolate and peanut butter. This always prompts the same puzzled reaction that I feel when I hear someone say they don't like Elvis. How is that even possible? The two are meant for each other.

CHOCOLATE PEANUT BUTTER PIE
with Candied Spicy Peanuts

MAKES ONE 9-INCH PIE

CRUST

5 tablespoons unsalted butter, melted, plus more for the pan

1½ cups chocolate graham cracker crumbs, from homemade cookies (see page 239) or store-bought

½ cup pretzels, finely chopped

½ cup roasted peanuts, finely chopped

2 tablespoons sugar

GANACHE

½ cup heavy cream

1 tablespoon honey

2 ounces semisweet chocolate, coarsely chopped

1 tablespoon unsalted butter, at room temperature

Pinch of kosher salt

CHOCOLATE PUDDING

½ cup whole milk

½ cup heavy cream

2 tablespoons sugar

Pinch of kosher salt

3 large egg yolks

4 ounces bittersweet chocolate, coarsely chopped

PEANUT BUTTER MOUSSE

¾ cup smooth peanut butter

4 ounces cream cheese, at room temperature

¼ cup sweetened condensed milk

¾ cup heavy cream

Candied Spicy Peanuts (recipe follows)

Make the crust: Heat the oven to 350°F. Butter a 9-inch pie pan.

Combine the cookie crumbs, pretzels, peanuts, sugar, and butter in a mixing bowl. Press the mixture into the bottom of the dish. Bake until light golden, about 10 minutes; set aside to cool.

Make the ganache: In a medium heavy saucepan, heat the cream and honey over medium-low heat, stirring, until the mixture is just barely at a simmer. Remove from the heat, add the chopped chocolate, and stir until smooth. Stir in the butter and salt and mix just to incorporate. Pour half of the ganache into the bottom of the prepared pie crust, creating a thin, even coating. Refrigerate the crust until you are ready to add the pudding layer. Reserve the remaining ganache in a bowl for the top of the pie.

(recipe continues)

Make the pudding: Heat the milk, cream, 1 tablespoon of the sugar, and the salt in a 2-quart saucepan over medium heat. In a separate bowl, mix together the egg yolks and remaining 1 tablespoon sugar. Temper the yolks by whisking one-third of the hot cream mixture into the yolks. Return the tempered egg mixture to the remaining hot cream in the saucepan and continue to cook over medium heat, stirring with a wooden spoon, until the mixture thickens enough to coat the back of the spoon. Remove from heat, add the chocolate, and stir until combined. Let cool for at least 10 minutes, stirring occasionally.

Pour the chocolate pudding on top of the ganache layer and refrigerate until set, at least 1 hour.

Make the peanut butter mousse: In the bowl of an electric mixer fitted with the paddle attachment, beat the peanut butter, cream cheese, and sweetened condensed milk until smooth. Transfer to another mixing bowl.

Using a clean bowl and the electric mixer fitted with the whisk attachment, whip the cream at medium-high speed until stiff peaks form, 3 to 4 minutes. Use a rubber spatula to fold half of the whipped cream into the peanut butter mixture. Then fold in the remaining whipped cream until well combined.

Top the pie with the mousse and chill for at least 1 more hour.

Slightly warm the remaining ganache (in the microwave or in the top of a double boiler) and pour over the top of the chilled mousse. Chill the pie in the refrigerator for at least 1 hour and up to 8 hours.

Sprinkle with candied peanuts before serving.

Chocolate Graham Crackers

MAKES 12 COOKIES, OR ABOUT 2½ CUPS CRUMBS

10 tablespoons unsalted butter, at room temperature

2 tablespoons packed dark brown sugar

2 tablespoons granulated sugar

2 tablespoons molasses

2 teaspoons honey

1 cup all-purpose flour, plus more for dusting

2 tablespoons whole wheat or whole wheat graham flour

2 tablespoons unsweetened cocoa powder

Pinch of kosher salt

Pinch of ground cinnamon

Pinch of ground ginger

Combine the butter, brown sugar, granulated sugar, cane syrup, and honey in an electric mixer fitted with the paddle attachment. Mix on medium speed until well incorporated, about 3 minutes. Use a rubber spatula to scrape down the sides of the bowl.

Reduce the speed to low and stir in both of the flours, the cocoa powder, salt, cinnamon, and ginger. Wrap the dough in plastic and refrigerate for at least 1 hour.

Heat the oven to 350°F. Line a baking sheet with parchment paper.

Dust a work surface lightly with flour, unwrap the dough, and roll, dusting with flour as needed, into an 8 × 12-inch rectangle that's ¼ inch thick. Brush off excess flour. Roll onto the rolling pin and unroll onto the baking sheet. Prick the dough all over using the tines of a fork. Cut into 12 rectangles, each 1½ inches × 3 inches.

Bake until crisp, 15 to 20 minutes. Allow the cookies to cool completely on the baking sheet before breaking into pieces. Store in an airtight container.

To make crumbs, pulse in a food processor.

Candied Spicy Peanuts

MAKES 1 CUP

1 large egg white

1 cup roasted, salted peanuts

¼ cup sugar

Pinch of ground cinnamon

Pinch of cayenne

Pinch of kosher salt

½ vanilla bean, split and scraped

Heat the oven to 350°F.

Lightly whisk the egg white in a large bowl. Add the peanuts, sugar, cinnamon, cayenne, salt, and the vanilla bean seeds and mix to combine. Spread the mixture on a baking sheet. Bake, using a metal spatula to stir the nuts every 5 minutes, until light golden, 20 minutes. Remove from the oven, set on a wire rack, and let the nuts cool completely.

Once cool, use a metal spatula to break them up on the baking sheet. Store the nuts in an airtight tin at room temperature for up to 2 weeks.

IN THE REALM of my cooking mentors and great culinary influences, there are acclaimed French chefs, Louisiana icons with some serious chops, and various relatives scattered throughout Acadiana. From the latter, few relatives have had more of an impact—aside from my grandad—than Aunt Sally, my mom's sister who currently lives in Robert's Cove. Her hands and palate have the assuredness and deftness that only comes from cooking for that kind of volume, for decades. Her sweets are unsurpassed and her coconut pie, in particular, is the stuff of legend in our family.

AUNT SALLY'S
Coconut Pie

MAKES ONE 9-INCH PIE

4 large eggs

1⅔ cups sugar

11 tablespoons unsalted butter, melted

1 tablespoon distilled white vinegar

1 teaspoon vanilla extract

1 cup sweetened shredded coconut

½ recipe Flaky Pie Crust, baked (recipe follows)

Heat the oven to 375°F.

Whisk the eggs, sugar, melted butter, vinegar, and vanilla in a large mixing bowl until well combined.

Scatter the coconut over the pie crust and pour the filling on top. Bake until the filling is set, about 30 minutes. Remove from the oven and allow the pie to completely cool on a wire rack before serving.

Flaky Pie Crust

MAKES TWO 9-INCH ROUNDS

12 tablespoons (1½ sticks) unsalted butter, cold, cut into pieces

½ cup rendered lard, cold

3 cups all-purpose flour, plus more for rolling

1 tablespoon sugar

1 teaspoon kosher salt

¼ teaspoon baking powder

Using your fingers, work the butter and lard into the flour, sugar, salt, and baking powder until the mixture has a mealy consistency. Add ½ cup ice cold water and mix until combined.

Divide the dough in half. Wrap and freeze half for up 2 months (defrost before rolling). Chill the other half for 30 minutes before rolling it out on a lightly floured work surface into a ¼-inch-thick circle; transfer to a 9-inch pie pan and trim the excess from around the edge. Prick holes in the bottom of the crust and then chill it in the freezer for 15 minutes.

While the crust chills, heat the oven to 350°F. Bake the crust until light golden, about 25 minutes. Cool completely before filling.

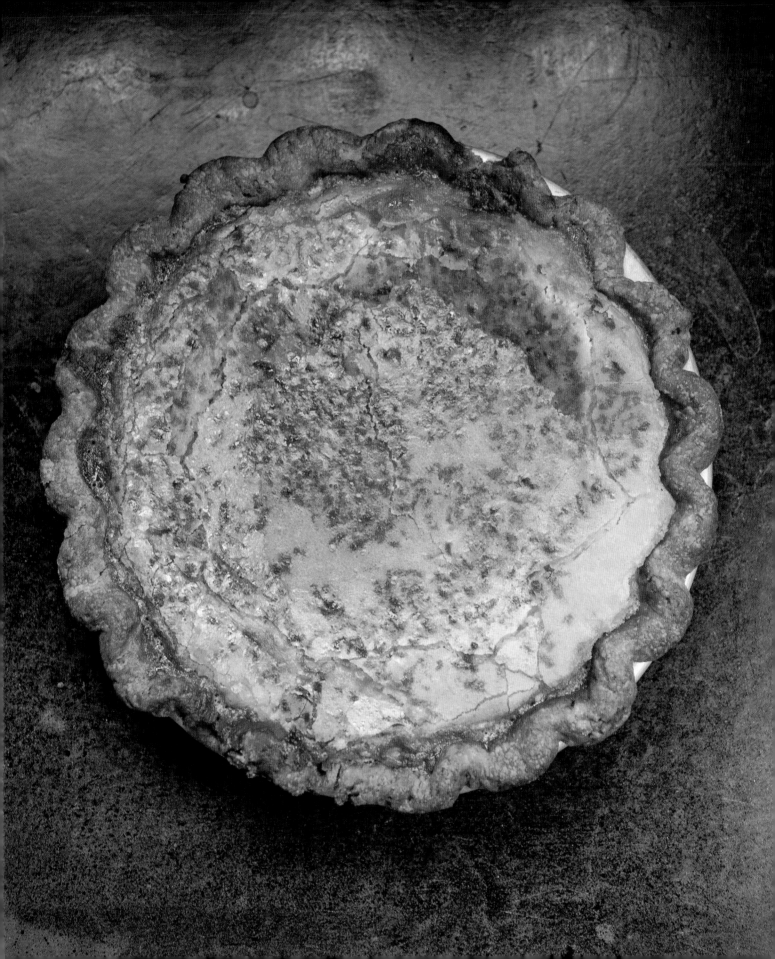

THERE'S NO DOUBT that this recipe takes some effort and planning, but the layers of flavors—a homemade chocolate cookie crust topped with a silky chocolate filling, a chocolate marshmallow topping, and homemade chocolate ice cream—make for a truly sublime experience. If you're short on time, you can make this using store-bought cookies and ice cream.

MISSISSIPPI MUD PIE
with Chocolate Graham Cracker Crust and Chocolate Ice Cream

MAKES ONE 9-INCH PIE

CHOCOLATE FILLING

6 tablespoons (¾ stick) unsalted butter

6 ounces semisweet chocolate, coarsely chopped

3 large eggs

Pinch of kosher salt

½ cup chopped pecans

Chocolate Graham Cracker Crust (recipe follows)

CHOCOLATE MARSHMALLOW TOPPING

2 heaping teaspoons unflavored gelatin

1 cup sugar

⅓ cup light corn syrup

2 tablespoons honey

3 tablespoons unsweetened cocoa powder

Chocolate Ice Cream (recipe follows)

Make the pie filling: Heat the oven to 325°F.

Melt the butter and chocolate in a double boiler or a bowl set over a saucepan of simmering water. Set aside to cool briefly.

In the bowl of an electric mixer fitted with the whisk attachment, whip the eggs and salt on medium-high speed until light and foamy, 5 minutes. Using a spatula, fold in the chocolate mixture. Add the pecans and stir to combine.

Transfer the filling to the prepared chocolate crust. Bake until set, 15 minutes. Cool completely on a wire rack.

Make the topping: Sprinkle the gelatin over ¼ cup cold water and let stand until all of the water is absorbed, 5 minutes. Melt over a hot water bath or in the microwave.

In a small, heavy saucepan heat the sugar, corn syrup, honey, and ¼ cup water to 242°F (use a candy thermometer). Remove from the heat and allow the sugar syrup to cool to 210°F. Pour the cooled syrup into the bowl of an electric mixer fitted with the whisk attachment and whip until light and foamy. Add the gelatin and whip until the mixture is light and fluffy, about 5 minutes.

Whisk in the cocoa powder, and then continue to whip on high speed until the mixture is light and fluffy and takes on a light cocoa color, 4 minutes. Let cool for 10 minutes.

Using a rubber spatula, spread the marshmallow mixture into the pie.

Using a kitchen torch, brown the topping until golden and then sprinkle with extra cookie crumbs. Alternatively, cover the edges of the pie with foil and brown briefly under the broiler—or you can skip this step entirely.

Serve the pie at room temperature or slightly warmed, with chocolate ice cream.

Chocolate Graham Cracker Crust

MAKES ONE 9-INCH PIE CRUST

2¼ cups chocolate graham cracker crumbs (see page 239)

2 tablespoons sugar

5 tablespoons unsalted butter, melted

Heat the oven to 350°F. Combine the crumbs, sugar, and butter and then press the mixture evenly into a 9-inch pie pan. Bake until fragrant and lightly toasted, about 10 minutes. Cool completely on a wire rack.

Chocolate Ice Cream

MAKES 2 QUARTS

1½ cups heavy cream

¼ cup plus 2 tablespoons whole milk

½ cup sugar

6 large egg yolks

Pinch of kosher salt

10 ounces bittersweet chocolate, coarsely chopped

1½ tablespoons coffee liqueur

If you're using a canister-style ice cream machine, freeze the canister for at least 12 hours or, preferably, for 24 hours.

In a heavy 2-quart saucepan, heat the cream, milk, and ¼ cup of the sugar, stirring, to scalding. In a separate bowl, whisk together the remaining ¼ cup sugar, the egg yolks, and salt. Temper the egg mixture by adding some of the hot milk to the yolks, whisking constantly, in a slow, steady stream. Transfer the egg mixture back to the saucepan and cook, stirring with a wooden spoon, until the custard thickens and coats the back of the spoon. Add the chocolate and mix well until fully melted. Strain the mixture into another container and chill completely for at least 2 hours, or overnight.

Stir in the coffee liqueur and freeze according to the manufacturer's directions, until the mixture has the texture of soft-serve ice cream. For a firmer texture, transfer to a covered plastic container and freeze for an additional 2 hours, or overnight.

IN MIDSUMMER IN Louisiana, when the massive fig trees are heavy with ripe, fragrant fruit, it's time to get busy. That's because fig season is a fleeting pleasure. Much of the fig crop is jarred and preserved, creating luscious jams to slather on toast and fold into pound cakes. I love how fresh figs caramelize in a sophisticated tart—especially when a brown butter custard is involved.

ROASTED FIG
Brown Butter Tart

MAKES ONE 9½-INCH TART

14 tablespoons (1¼ sticks) unsalted butter

3 large egg yolks

½ cup sugar

½ vanilla bean, split and scraped

⅛ teaspoon ground cinnamon

⅛ teaspoon ground nutmeg

Pinch of ground ginger

⅛ teaspoon kosher salt

1 tablespoon grated orange or lemon zest

3 tablespoons all-purpose flour

Sweet Dough Crust, prebaked (page 248)

1 pint fresh figs, quartered

Cinnamon Sugar (page 231)

Heat the oven to 325°F.

Heat the butter in a small saucepan over medium heat until the butter foams and then subsides. The butter should have a nutty aroma and a dark golden color. Remove from the heat and set on a cool surface to help stop the cooking.

In a medium bowl, beat the egg yolks and sugar. Add the vanilla bean seeds, cinnamon, nutmeg, ginger, salt, and zest and stir to combine. Whisking constantly, slowly and carefully pour in the warm browned butter. Sift the flour over the mixture and stir until just combined (do not overmix).

Pour the mixture into the cooled tart shell and spread evenly. Top with the figs and sprinkle with cinnamon sugar. Bake until the filling is completely set, 40 minutes.

Cool to room temperature and serve.

I CAN'T THINK about blackberries without feeling that first wave of Southern summer heat on the back of my neck, with a memory of standing along some country road, carefully picking the plump berries from a massive tangle of treacherous sticker bushes and vines. The reward of those ripe berries is totally worth enduring the finger scrapes, pricks, and dusty sweat.

In this recipe, juicy sweet berries are topped with a cloud of subtly sweet, tangy mascarpone to create decadent little tartlets that are as pretty as they are sublime to eat. This is my ideal dessert because the layers are simple and deliver pure flavors—flaky pastry, luscious cream, fruit at the peak of its season. Make these tarts in midsummer, when the fat Southern blackberries are impossibly sweet.

LEMON BLACKBERRY TARTLET
with Sweet Mascarpone

MAKES EIGHT 4-INCH TARTLETS (OR ONE 10-INCH TART)

½ recipe Sweet Dough Crust (recipe follows), baked in eight 4-inch tartlet shells or one 10-inch tart pan

5 tablespoons unsalted butter, at room temperature

1⅓ cups plus 1 tablespoon sugar

Grated zest from 2 lemons

4 large eggs

⅓ cup plus 1 tablespoon and 1 teaspoon all purpose flour

¼ teaspoon kosher salt

½ teaspoon vanilla extract

1 pint blackberries

8 ounces mascarpone

Confectioners' sugar, for garnish

Heat the oven to 325°F.

In the bowl of an electric mixer fitted with the paddle attachment, beat the butter, 1⅓ cups of the sugar, and the lemon zest until light and fluffy. Add the eggs one at a time, scraping the sides of the bowl after each egg. Add the flour, salt, and vanilla and mix until just combined.

Divide the blackberries among the tartlet shells and top each crust with the lemon mixture, being careful not to overfill. Bake until the top is golden brown and the custard has set, 15 to 20 minutes for tartlets and 25 to 30 minutes for one big tart. Let cool completely before carefully turning them out of tartlet pans, or slicing the large tart.

To serve, combine the mascarpone and the remaining tablespoon sugar in a small bowl. Serve each tartlet or tart slice with a dusting of confectioners' sugar and a dollop of sweetened mascarpone.

Sweet Dough Crust

**MAKES TWO 9½- TO 10-INCH TARTS
OR SIXTEEN 4-INCH TARTLETS**

12 tablespoons (1½ sticks) unsalted
    butter, at room temperature

½ cup plus 1 tablespoon sugar

½ teaspoon kosher salt

2 large eggs

2 large yolks

½ teaspoon vanilla extract

3½ cups all-purpose flour, plus more
    for rolling

In the bowl of an electric mixer fitted with the paddle attachment, beat the butter, sugar, and salt until fluffy. Add the eggs and yolks one at a time, beating until incorporated and scraping down the bowl after each addition. Mix in the vanilla. Add the flour and mix slowly just until incorporated. Do not overmix. Transfer the dough to a work surface, divide the dough in half, and wrap each half in plastic. Refrigerate for at least 1 hour or overnight. Freeze half for another use for up to 2 months (defrost before rolling).

Heat the oven to 350°F.

On a lightly floured work surface, roll half of the dough into a ¼-inch-thick round. Use the rolling pin to transfer the round into the tart pan. Use your fingers to press the dough evenly into the pan and then use the rolling pin to roll over the pan and trim off any excess. Use a fork to prick holes in the bottom of the crust; refrigerate for 10 to 15 minutes.

Bake the crust until light golden, about 15 minutes. Cool completely on a wire rack before filling.

THE TIMELESS APPEAL OF SUGAR

I don't think I ever realized the power of sweets—and their dizzying effect on children—until a recent visit from my aunt Sally. As parents we try very hard to limit the amount of sugar that our kids consume. Then Aunt Sally shows up like Santa, with gobs of candied pecans, coconut and pecan pie, cookies, Cokes, and so on.

At first I was shocked, and not entirely pleased, at the amount of sugar that had overtaken my house. And then I noticed how delighted the kids were, with their fingers in cookie jars, creamy custard, and chocolate, and my childhood started rushing back to me. I remembered the anticipation of going to different family members' homes, knowing that something sweet awaited us. A tray of cookies or a tin of candy transformed what would normally be a *boring adult get-together* into an exciting party brimming with desserts.

For the most part, I still try to make healthy choices for my children, but every now and then I think about Aunt Sally and the pleasure of cookie jars and dessert tables and realize it's time to make a batch of cookies or brownies—and pretend that they're for my kids.

Acknowledgments

Ryan Prewitt, my partner at Pêche, for working by my side developing and testing these recipes, and for excellent company during countless hours by the smoker.

Paula Disbrowe for all her diligence in keeping the book focused and helping me see the path.

Chris Granger for tireless work to get the best shot every time, while the rest of us were scalloping and shotgunning beer.

Janis Donnaud for persuading me to write this book.

Rhonda Ruckman, my pastry chef for Link Restaurants, for all her work and for being the best pastry chef I could imagine.

Rica Allannic for her patience and allowing me to find my own voice for this book.

Julia Reed. First off for being Julia Reed. For being such a great Southerner and great friend, and for brilliant parties.

Jimmy Buffett for being an inspiration to me for Gulf Coast lifestyle, history, culture, and a sense of belonging and place.

Nick Pihakis for starting Fatback with me, and for being one of the funnest and smartest people I know.

To the entire Fatback Collective for all the cookouts, good times, and raucous, loud bus rides in the middle of the night.

My dad for all the fishing trips.

And to my wife, Amanda, for her patience and support while I traveled around the South and beyond for this book.

Index

Note: Page references in *italics* indicate recipe photographs.

Absinthe
    Copperhead, 27
Alabama White Barbecue Sauce, 71
Almonds
    Holiday Shortbread with Lemon Icing, *218*, 219
Antiguan Julep, 30
Appetizers
    Beach House Ceviche, *148*, 149
    Beef Tenderloin and Yeast Rolls with Horseradish Cream Sauce, 58, *61*
    Black Pepper Biscuits with Country Ham and Hot Mustard Sauce, 56
    Blue Crab Beignets with White Rémoulade Sauce, 54, *54*
    Cajun-Spiced Soda Crackers, 48
    Chicken Liver Pâté, 44
    Crab Louis with Toast Points, 39
    Crawfish and Spring Onion Gratin, 152
    Creamy Onion Dip, *42*, 43
    Fancy Spiced Pecans, 38
    Fried Country Terrine, 126–27, *127*
    Grilled Scallops with Green Garlic Butter, 156, *157*
    Herbsaint Headcheese, 114–15
    New Orleans Barbecue Shrimp, 162, *163*
    Parmesan Bacon Gougères, *50*, 51
    Pork Rillons, 120, *121*
    Scallop Crudo with Tomatoes, Lemon, and Basil, *154*, 155
    Shrimp Rémoulade, 52, *52*
    Smoked Mullet Dip, *158*, 159
    Southern Bruschetta with Bacon and Tomato, 47
    Spicy Cheddar Crackers, 49
    Spicy Roasted Peanuts, 36, *37*
    Sweet and Sour Onion Jam, 46
    Uruguayan Spicy Baked Cheese, 40, *41*
Apple
    Pecan Bread, Spiced, 230–31
    Slaw, Gingered, 188, *189*
Arugula and Parmesan, Grilled Pork Tenderloins with, 78
Aunt Sally's Coconut Pie, 240, *241*

Bacon
    Chicken Liver Pâté, 44
    Guanciale, 128
    Parmesan Gougères, *50*, 51
    and Tomato, Southern Bruschetta with, 47
Banana Pudding with Moonshine Whipped Cream, *234*, 235–36
Bars
    Heath Bar Brownies with Fudgy Chocolate Icing, 226–27, *227*
    Orange Cream Cheese, with Shortbread Crust, *228*, 229
    White Chocolate Macadamia Blondies, 223
Bean(s)
    Pork Belly and Smoked Sausage Cassoulet, 106–7, *107*
    Red, and Rice, Monday, 133
    White, and Tasso Gratin, 204
Beef
    Short Ribs, Beer-Smoked, 88, *89*
    Short Rib Sugo, *136*, 137
    Tenderloin and Yeast Rolls with Horseradish Cream Sauce, 58, *61*
Beer-Smoked Beef Short Ribs, 88, *89*
Beignets, Blue Crab, with White Rémoulade Sauce, 54, *54*
Beurre Blanc, 146
Bing Cherry and White Chocolate Bread Pudding, 233
Biscuits, Black Pepper, with Country Ham and Hot Mustard Sauce, 56
Blackberry Lemon Tartlet with Sweet Mascarpone, 246, *247*
Blondies, White Chocolate Macadamia, 223
Blueberry(ies)
    Chuck Berry, 19
    Syrup, 19
Bourbon
    Banana Pudding with Moonshine Whipped Cream, *234*, 235–36
    Cherry Bounce, 21
    Deer Stand Old-Fashioned, 31
    Free Cochon Payton, 21
    King Street Derby, 25
    Louisiana Hayride, 20
    note about, 15
Bread Pudding, Bing Cherry and White Chocolate, 233
Breads
    Apple Pecan, Spiced, 230–31
    Black Pepper Biscuits with Country Ham and Hot Mustard Sauce, 56
    Savory Sausage and Cheese Rolls, 119
    Sherry Prewitt's Yeast Rolls, 60–61, *61*
    Southern Bruschetta with Bacon and Tomato, 47
    Zucchini Walnut, 232
Breakfast Sausage, 118
Brittle, Peanut, 215

Broccoli, I-talian Style, 198, *198*
Brownies, Heath Bar, with Fudgy Chocolate Icing, 226–27, *227*
Bruschetta, Southern, with Bacon and Tomato, 47

Cajun Macaroni Salad, 199
Cajun-Spiced Soda Crackers, 48
Caramel, Salted, Peanut Brittle Ice Cream, 214–15
Carrot Raisin Salad, 186, *187*
Cassoulet, Pork Belly and Smoked Sausage, 106–7, *107*
Catfish Court Bouillon, 160–61
Cauliflower and Gruyère Gratin, 200, 201
Ceviche, Beach House, *148*, 149
Champagne
    Cocktail, Herbsaint, 18
    Meyer Lemon French 75, 16, *17*
Cheese
    Cauliflower and Gruyère Gratin, *200*, 201
    Crawfish and Spring Onion Gratin, 152
    Cream, Orange Bars with Shortbread Crust, *228*, 229
    Grilled Pork Tenderloins with Arugula and Parmesan, 78
    Lemon Blackberry Tartlet with Sweet Mascarpone, 246, *247*
    Parmesan Bacon Gougères, *50*, 51
    and Sausage Rolls, Savory, 119
    Spicy Cheddar Crackers, 49
    Spring Peas with Feta and Mint, 191
    Sweet Potato Gratin, 205
    Uruguayan Spicy Baked, 40, *41*
Cherry(ies)
    Bing, and White Chocolate

Cherries (continued)
    Bread Pudding, 233
    Bounce, 21
    Free Cochon Payton, 21
Chicken
    Braised, with Salami and
        Olives, *94*, 95
    Breasts, Grilled, with Lemon-
        Olive Vinaigrette, 72
    Chivito Sandwich with Ham
        and Olive Spread, *64*, 69
    Grilled, on a Stick with
        Alabama White Barbecue
        Sauce, 70, *71*
    Liver Pâté, 44
    Smothered, 97
    Thighs, Smoked, 73
Chile(s)
    Beach House Ceviche, *148*, 149
    Crab Louis with Toast Points,
        39
    and Kumquats, Butter and
        Olive Oil–Poached Tuna
        with, 176
    and Kumquats, Slow-Roasted
        Pork Shoulder with, 100, *101*
    Pickled, Vinegar, Easy, 169
Chocolate
    Chubbies, Triple-Chip, 222
    Chunk, Extra-Bittersweet,
        Monster Cookies, McGaws',
        224, 225
    Graham Cracker Crust, 243
    Graham Crackers, 239
    Heath Bar Brownies with
        Fudgy Chocolate Icing,
        226–27, *227*
    Ice Cream, 243
    Icing, Fudgy, 227
    Peanut Butter Pie with
        Candied Spiced Peanuts,
        237–38
    Sea Salt Turtles, 210
    White, and Bing Cherry Bread
        Pudding, 233
    White, Macadamia Blondies,
        223
Chuck Berry, 19
Cinnamon
    Simple Syrup, 20

Sugar, 231
A Clockwork Orange, 24
Coconut Pie, Aunt Sally's, 240,
    241
Collard Green Slaw, 190
Cookies
    Chocolate Graham Crackers,
        239
    Extra-Bittersweet Chocolate
        Chunk Monster, McGaws',
        224, 225
    Holiday Shortbread with
        Lemon Icing, *218*, 219
    Shortbread, 221
    Triple-Chip Chocolate
        Chubbies, 222
    Vanilla Wafers, 236
    Zucker Platschen (German
        Sugar Cookies), 216, *217*
Copperhead, 27
Cornmeal
    Delta Shrimp Tamales, 125
    and Pork Tamales, Rich, *122*,
        123
Court Bouillon, Catfish, 160–61
Couscous, Fresh Mint, 195, *195*
Crab(meat)
    Blue, Beignets with White
        Rémoulade Sauce, 54, *54*
    Louis with Toast Points, 39
    and Shrimp Spaghetti, 150,
        151
    Soft-Shell, Meunière, 170
    and Spinach Dumplings, 144,
        145
    Stone, Claws with Easy
        Pickled Chile Vinegar, *168*,
        169
    Watermelon Gazpacho with,
        147
Crackers
    Soda, Cajun-Spiced, 48
    Spicy Cheddar, 49
Crawfish and Spring Onion
    Gratin, 152
Cream Soda Sherbet, *212*, 213
Crusts
    Chocolate Graham Cracker,
        243
    Pie, Flaky, 240

Sweet Dough, 248
Cucumbers
    Beach House Ceviche, *148*,
        149
    Yogurt Sauce, and Mint,
        Braised and Crispy Goat
        with, 108–9, *109*
Curaçao
    Antiguan Julep, 30
Curry Powder, Homemade, 186

Deer Stand Old-Fashioned, 31
Delta Shrimp Tamales, 125
Desserts
    Aunt Sally's Coconut Pie,
        240, *241*
    Banana Pudding with
        Moonshine Whipped Cream,
        234, 235–36
    Bing Cherry and White
        Chocolate Bread Pudding,
        233
    Chocolate Graham Crackers,
        239
    Chocolate Peanut Butter
        Pie with Candied Spiced
        Peanuts, 237–38
    Cream Soda Sherbet, *212*, 213
    Grapefruit and Mint Granita,
        211
    Heath Bar Brownies with
        Fudgy Chocolate Icing,
        226–27, *227*
    Holiday Shortbread with
        Lemon Icing, *218*, 219
    Lemon Blackberry Tartlet
        with Sweet Mascarpone,
        246, *247*
    McGaws' Extra-Bittersweet
        Chocolate Chunk Monster
        Cookies, *224*, 225
    Mississippi Mud Pie with
        Chocolate Graham Cracker
        Crust and Chocolate Ice
        Cream, 242–43
    Orange Cream Cheese Bars
        with Shortbread Crust, *228*,
        229
    Roasted Fig Brown Butter
        Tart, *244*, 245

Salted Caramel Peanut Brittle
    Ice Cream, 214–15
Sea Salt Turtles, 210
Shortbread Cookies, 221
Triple-Chip Chocolate
    Chubbies, 222
Vanilla Wafers, 236
White Chocolate Macadamia
    Blondies, 223
Zucker Platschen (German
    Sugar Cookies), 216, *217*
Dips and spreads
    Creamy Onion Dip, *42*, 43
    Olive Spread, 69
    Pork Rillons, 120, *121*
    Smoked Mullet Dip, *158*, 159
    Sweet and Sour Onion Jam,
        46
    Uruguayan Spicy Baked
        Cheese, 40, *41*
    White Rémoulade Sauce, 55
Drinks. *See also* Syrups
    Antiguan Julep, 30
    Chuck Berry, 19
    A Clockwork Orange, 24
    Copperhead, 27
    Deer Stand Old-Fashioned, 31
    Flora-bama Rum Punch,
        22, *22*
    Free Cochon Payton, 21
    Herbsaint Champagne
        Cocktail, 18
    Julia Reed's Scotch Old-
        Fashioned, *28*, 29
    King Street Derby, 25
    Louisiana Hayride, 20
    Meyer Lemon French 75,
        16, *17*
    St. Edwards No. 1, 26
Duck
    Braised, Hunter's Style,
        98–99
    Smoked, with Aromatic Salt, 74
Dumplings, Crab and Spinach,
    144, *145*

Eggplant
    Marinated, with Chile Flakes
        and Mint, 194
    salting, before cooking, 194

Eggs
    Chicken Chivito Sandwich
      with Ham and Olive Spread,
      64, 69
    Fried, and Pork Jowls,
      Spaghetti with, 134, 135

Fig(s)
    Grilled Pork Chops with
      Sweet and Sour Dried Fruit,
      79
    Roasted, Brown Butter Tart,
      244, 245
Fish. *See also* Shellfish
    Beach House Ceviche, *148*,
      149
    Broiled Flounder with Cherry
      Tomatoes and Basil, 175
    Butter and Olive Oil–Poached
      Tuna with Kumquats and
      Chiles, 176
    Catfish Court Bouillon,
      160–61
    Collars, Fried, with Chile
      Vinegar, *116*, 117
    Salt-Crusted Red Snapper,
      177, *179*
    Smoked Mullet Dip, *158*,
      159
Flora-bama Rum Punch, 22, *22*
Flounder, Broiled, with Cherry
    Tomatoes and Basil, 175
Free Cochon Payton, 21
Frog Legs, Crisp Fried, 171
Fruit. *See also specific fruits*
    Dried, Sweet and Sour, Grilled
      Pork Chops with, 79

Garlic
    Green, Butter, Grilled
      Scallops with, 156, *157*
    I-talian Style Broccoli, 198,
      198
    Salsa Verde, 179
Gazpacho, Watermelon, with
    Crabmeat, 147
Gin
    Meyer Lemon French 75,
      16, *17*
    St. Edwards No. 1, 26

Gingered Apple Slaw, 188, *189*
Goat, Braised and Crispy, with
    Yogurt Sauce, Cucumbers,
    and Mint, 108–9, *109*
Gougères, Parmesan Bacon,
    50, 51
Graham Cracker(s)
    Chocolate, 239
    Chocolate, Crust, 243
Grains
    Delta Shrimp Tamales, 125
    Monday Red Beans and Rice,
      133
    Rich Pork and Cornmeal
      Tamales, *122*, 123
    Smoked Ham and Rice Salad,
      196, *197*
Grand Marnier
    A Clockwork Orange, 24
Granita, Grapefruit and Mint, 211
Grapefruit
    King Street Derby, 25
    and Mint Granita, 211
Green Garlic Butter, Grilled
    Scallops with, 156, *157*
Green(s)
    Collard, Slaw, 190
    Crab and Spinach Dumplings,
      144, *145*
    Crab Louis with Toast Points,
      39
    Grilled Pork Tenderloins
      with Arugula and Parmesan,
      78
    Shrimp Rémoulade, 52, *52*
Grilling, primer on, 68
Grouper
    Beach House Ceviche, *148*,
      149
Guanciale, 128
Guinea Hen Gumbo, 96

Ham
    Country, and Hot Mustard
      Sauce, Black Pepper Biscuits
      with, 56
    country, buying, 57
    Fresh, Brined, 129
    Hocks and Crowder Peas,
      202, *203*

Monday Red Beans and
    Rice, 133
    and Olive Spread, Chivito
      Sandwich with, 64, 69
    Smoked, and Rice Salad,
      196, *197*
    Steak, Grilled, with Charred
      Blood Oranges, 80, 81
    Tupelo Honey–Glazed, 103
Headcheese, Herbsaint, 114–15
Heath Bar Brownies with Fudgy
    Chocolate Icing, 226–27,
    227
Herbs. *See also* Mint
    Salsa Verde, 179
Herbsaint Champagne Cocktail,
    18
Herbsaint Headcheese, 114–15
Holiday Shortbread with Lemon
    Icing, *218*, 219
Honey
    Syrup, 31
    Tupelo, –Glazed Ham, 103
Horseradish Cream Sauce, 58

Ice Cream
    Chocolate, 243
    Salted Caramel Peanut
      Brittle, 214–15
Icing
    Chocolate, Fudgy, 227
    Lemon, 221

Jam, Sweet and Sour Onion, 46
Julia Reed's Scotch Old-
    Fashioned, *28*, 29

King Street Derby, 25
Kumquats
    and Chiles, Butter and Olive
      Oil–Poached Tuna with, 176
    and Chiles, Slow-Roasted
      Pork Shoulder with, 100, *101*

Lamb
    Leg of, Roast, with Texas
      Campfire Dry Rub, 84, *85*
    Neck, Crispy, 138, 139
    Saddle, Grilled Boneless,
      82, 83

Shoulder Stew with Lemons
    and Olives, 102
Lemon
    Blackberry Tartlet with Sweet
      Mascarpone, 246, *247*
    Icing, 221
    Meyer, French 75, 16, *17*
    -Olive Vinaigrette, 72
Lettuce
    Crab Louis with Toast Points,
      39
    Shrimp Rémoulade, 52, *52*
Liver, Chicken, Pâté, 44
Louisiana Hayride, 20

Macadamia Blondies, White
    Chocolate, 223
Main dishes
    Beef Short Rib Sugo, *136*, 137
    Beer-Smoked Beef Short
      Ribs, 88, *89*
    Braised and Crispy Goat with
      Yogurt Sauce, Cucumbers,
      and Mint, 108–9, *109*
    Braised Chicken with Salami
      and Olives, 94, 95
    Brined Fresh Ham, 129
    Broiled Flounder with Cherry
      Tomatoes and Basil, 175
    Butter and Olive Oil–Poached
      Tuna with Kumquats and
      Chiles, 176
    Catfish Court Bouillon,
      160–61
    Chicken Chivito Sandwich
      with Ham and Olive Spread,
      64, 69
    Crisp Fried Frog Legs, 171
    Crispy Lamb Neck, 138, *139*
    Crispy Pork Cutlets with
      Brown Butter, Lemon, and
      Sage, *104*, 105
    Delta Shrimp Tamales, 125
    Fried Fish Collars with Chile
      Vinegar, *116*, 117
    Grilled Boneless Lamb Saddle,
      82, 83
    Grilled Chicken Breasts with
      Lemon-Olive Vinaigrette,
      72

Main Dishes *(continued)*
  Grilled Chicken on a Stick
    with Alabama White
    Barbecue Sauce, 70, *71*
  Grilled Ham Steak with
    Charred Blood Oranges,
    80, 81
  Grilled Pork Chops with
    Sweet and Sour Dried Fruit,
    79
  Grilled Pork Tenderloins with
    Arugula and Parmesan, 78
  Guinea Hen Gumbo, 96
  Hot Coal-Fired Royal Reds,
    166, *167*
  Hunter's Style Braised Duck,
    98–99
  Lamb Shoulder Stew with
    Lemons and Olives, 102
  Mamou Grilled Pork Steak
    Sandwich, 76, *77*
  Monday Red Beans and Rice,
    133
  Pork Belly and Smoked
    Sausage Cassoulet, 106–7,
    107
  Pork Neck Bone Stew, 132
  Rich Pork and Cornmeal
    Tamales, *122*, 123
  Roast Leg of Lamb with Texas
    Campfire Dry Rub, 84, *85*
  Royal Red Shrimp, *164*, 165
  Salt-Crusted Red Snapper,
    177, *179*
  Shrimp and Crab Spaghetti,
    150, *151*
  Slow-Roasted Pork Shoulder
    with Kumquats and Chiles,
    100, *101*
  Smoked Chicken Thighs, 73
  Smoked Duck with Aromatic
    Salt, 74
  Smothered Chicken, 97
  Soft-Shell Crabs Meunière,
    170
  Spaghetti with Pork Jowls and
    Fried Eggs, 134, *135*
  Spicy Grilled Quail with
    Grilled Peaches, 75
  Stone Crab Claws with Easy

  Pickled Chile Vinegar, *168*,
    169
  Tupelo Honey–Glazed Ham,
    103
  Turkey Noodle Soup, 130–31,
    131
Mamou Grilled Pork Steak
  Sandwich, 76, *77*
McGaws' Extra-Bittersweet
  Chocolate Chunk Monster
  Cookies, *224*, 225
Meat. *See also* Lamb; Pork
  Beef Short Rib Sugo, *136*, 137
  Beef Tenderloin and Yeast
    Rolls with Horseradish
    Cream Sauce, 58, *61*
  Beer-Smoked Beef Short
    Ribs, 88, *89*
  Braised and Crispy Goat with
    Yogurt Sauce, Cucumbers,
    and Mint, 108–9, *109*
Melon. *See* Watermelon
Meunière Sauce, 170
Meyer Lemon French 75, 16, *17*
Mint
  Antiguan Julep, 30
  and Chile Flakes, Marinated
    Eggplant with, 194
  Couscous, Fresh, 195, *195*
  and Feta, Spring Peas with, 191
  and Grapefruit Granita, 211
Mississippi Mud Pie with
  Chocolate Graham Cracker
  Crust and Chocolate Ice
  Cream, 242–43
Moonshine Whipped Cream,
  Banana Pudding with, *234*,
  235–36
Mullet, Smoked, Dip, *158*, 159
Mushrooms
  Beef Short Rib Sugo, *136*, 137
  Hunter's Style Braised Duck,
    98–99
Mustard
  -Marinated Turnips, 192
  Sauce, Hot, 57

Noodle Soup, Turkey, 130–31, *131*
Nuts. *See also* Peanut(s);
  Pecan(s)

Holiday Shortbread with
  Lemon Icing, *218*, 219
McGaws' Extra-Bittersweet
  Chocolate Chunk Monster
  Cookies, *224*, 225
White Chocolate Macadamia
  Blondies, 223
Zucchini Walnut Bread, 232

Olive(s)
  and Lemons, Lamb Shoulder
    Stew with, 102
  -Lemon Vinaigrette, 72
  and Salami, Braised Chicken
    with, *94*, 95
  Spread, 69
Onion(s)
  Dip, Creamy, *42*, 43
  Jam, Sweet and Sour, 46
  Spring, and Crawfish Gratin,
    152
  Spring, Sweet and Sour, 193,
    193
Orange(s)
  Blood, Charred, Grilled Ham
    Steak with, *80*, 81
  A Clockwork Orange, 24
  Cream Cheese Bars with
    Shortbread Crust, *228*,
    229

Parmesan Bacon Gougères,
  50, 51
Pasta and noodles
  Cajun Macaroni Salad, 199
  Shrimp and Crab Spaghetti,
    150, *151*
  Spaghetti with Pork Jowls and
    Fried Eggs, 134, *135*
  Turkey Noodle Soup, 130–31,
    131
Pâté, Chicken Liver, 44
Pâté Spice, 45
Peaches, Grilled, Spicy Grilled
  Quail with, 75
Peanut Butter
  Chocolate Pie with Candied
    Spiced Peanuts, 237–38
  Salted Caramel Peanut Brittle
    Ice Cream, 214–15

Peanut(s)
  Brittle, 215
  Candied Spicy, 239
  Sea Salt Turtles, 210
  Spicy Roasted, 36, *37*
Peas
  Crowder, and Ham Hocks,
    202, *203*
  Spring, with Feta and Mint, 191
Pecan(s)
  Apple Bread, Spiced, 230–31
  Deer Stand Old-Fashioned, 31
  Fancy Spiced, 38
  Sea Salt Turtles, 210
Peppers. *See* Chile(s)
Pie Crusts
  Chocolate Graham Cracker,
    243
  Flaky, 240
  Sweet Dough Crust, 248
Pies
  Chocolate Peanut Butter,
    with Candied Spiced
    Peanuts, 237–38
  Coconut, Aunt Sally's, 240,
    241
  Mississippi Mud, with
    Chocolate Graham Cracker
    Crust and Chocolate Ice
    Cream, 242–43
Pork. *See also* Bacon; Ham;
  Sausage(s)
  Belly and Smoked Sausage
    Cassoulet, 106–7, *107*
  Breakfast Sausage, 118
  Chops, Grilled, with Sweet
    and Sour Dried Fruit, 79
  and Cornmeal Tamales, Rich,
    122, 123
  Cutlets, Crispy, with Brown
    Butter, Lemon, and Sage,
    104, 105
  Fried Country Terrine,
    126–27, *127*
  Guanciale, 128
  Herbsaint Headcheese,
    114–15
  Jowls and Fried Eggs,
    Spaghetti with, 134, *135*
  Neck Bone Stew, 132

Rillons, 120, *121*
Shoulder, Slow-Roasted,
    with Kumquats and Chiles,
    100, *101*
Steak, Grilled, Sandwich,
    Mamou, 76, *77*
Tasso and White Bean Gratin,
    204
Tenderloins, Grilled, with
    Arugula and Parmesan, 78
Potato, Sweet, Gratin, 205
Poultry and game birds. *See also*
    Chicken
Guinea Hen Gumbo, 96
Hunter's Style Braised Duck,
    98–99
Smoked Duck with Aromatic
    Salt, 74
Spicy Grilled Quail with
    Grilled Peaches, 75
Turkey Noodle Soup, 130–31,
    131
Pudding
Banana, with Moonshine
    Whipped Cream, *234*,
    235–36
Bread, Bing Cherry and White
    Chocolate, 233

Quail, Spicy Grilled, with Grilled
    Peaches, 75

Raisin(s)
Carrot Salad, 186, *187*
Grilled Pork Chops with
    Sweet and Sour Dried Fruit,
    79
Red Snapper, Salt-Crusted,
    177, *179*
Rémoulade Sauce, 53
Rémoulade Sauce, White, 55
Rice
Red Beans and, Monday, 133
and Smoked Ham Salad, 196,
    197
Rolls
Savory Sausage and Cheese,
    119
Yeast, Sherry Prewitt's,
    60–61, *61*

Rub, Dry, Texas Campfire, 85
Rum
Antiguan Julep, 30
Punch, Flora-bama, 22, *22*
Rye
Copperhead, 27

Salads
Carrot Raisin, 186, *187*
Collard Green Slaw, 190
Gingered Apple Slaw, 188, *189*
Macaroni, Cajun, 199
Smoked Ham and Rice, 196,
    197
Salami and Olives, Braised
    Chicken with, *94*, 95
Salsa Verde, 179
Salted Caramel Peanut Brittle
    Ice Cream, 214–15
Sandwiches
Chicken Chivito, with Ham
    and Olive Spread, *64*, 69
Grilled Pork Steak, Mamou,
    76, *77*
Sauces
Alabama White Barbecue, 71
Beef Short Rib Sugo, *136*, 137
Beurre Blanc, 146
Horseradish Cream, 58
Hot Mustard, 57
Meunière, 170
Rémoulade, 53
Rémoulade, White, 55
Salsa Verde, 179
Sausage(s)
Braised Chicken with Salami
    and Olives, *94*, 95
Breakfast, 118
and Cheese Rolls, Savory, 119
Guinea Hen Gumbo, 96
Monday Red Beans and Rice,
    133
Pork Neck Bone Stew, 132
Smoked, and Pork Belly
    Cassoulet, 106–7, *107*
Scallop(s)
Crudo with Tomatoes, Lemon,
    and Basil, *154*, 155
Grilled, with Green Garlic
    Butter, 156, *157*

Scotch Old-Fashioned, Julia
    Reed's, 28, *29*
Seafood. *See also* Crab(meat);
    Fish; Shrimp
Crawfish and Spring Onion
    Gratin, 152
Crisp Fried Frog Legs, 171
Grilled Scallops with Green
    Garlic Butter, 156, *157*
Scallop Crudo with Tomatoes,
    Lemon, and Basil, *154*, 155
Sea Salt Turtles, 210
Shallots
Sweet and Sour Onion Jam,
    46
Shellfish. *See also* Crab(meat);
    Shrimp
Crawfish and Spring Onion
    Gratin, 152
Grilled Scallops with Green
    Garlic Butter, 156, *157*
Scallop Crudo with Tomatoes,
    Lemon, and Basil, *154*, 155
Sherbet, Cream Soda, *212*, 213
Shortbread
Cookies, 221
Holiday, with Lemon Icing,
    218, 219
Shrimp
Barbecue, New Orleans,
    162, *163*
Beach House Ceviche, *148*,
    149
and Crab Spaghetti, 150, *151*
Rémoulade, 52, *52*
Royal Red, *164*, 165
Royal Reds, Hot Coal-Fired,
    166, *167*
Tamales, Delta, 125
Sides
Cajun Macaroni Salad, 199
Carrot Raisin Salad, 186, *187*
Cauliflower and Gruyère
    Gratin, *200*, 201
Collard Green Slaw, 190
Fresh Mint Couscous, 195,
    195
Gingered Apple Slaw, 188, *189*
Ham Hocks and Crowder
    Peas, 202, *203*

I-talian Style Broccoli, 198,
    198
Marinated Eggplant with
    Chile Flakes and Mint, 194
Mustard-Marinated Turnips,
    192
Smoked Ham and Rice Salad,
    196, *197*
Spring Peas with Feta and
    Mint, 191
Sweet and Sour Spring
    Onions, 193, *193*
Sweet Potato Gratin, 205
Tasso and White Bean Gratin,
    204
Simple Syrup
Basic, 17
Cinnamon, 20
Rich Demerara, 30
Soda Crackers, Cajun-Spiced, 48
Soups. *See also* Stews
Turkey Noodle, 130–31, *131*
Soups (continued)
Watermelon Gazpacho with
    Crabmeat, 147
Southern Bruschetta with Bacon
    and Tomato, 47
Sparkling wine
Chuck Berry, 19
Herbsaint Champagne
    Cocktail, 18
Meyer Lemon French 75,
    16, *17*
Spinach and Crab Dumplings,
    144, *145*
Spring Onion(s)
and Crawfish Gratin, 152
Sweet and Sour, 193, *193*
St. Edwards No. 1, 26
St. Germain
Chuck Berry, 19
St. Edwards No. 1, 26
Stews
Guinea Hen Gumbo, 96
Lamb Shoulder, with Lemons
    and Olives, 102
Stews (continued)
Pork Neck Bone, 132
Sugar, Cinnamon, 231
Sweet and Sour Onion Jam, 46

Sweet and Sour Spring Onions, 193, *193*
Sweet Potato Gratin, 205
Syrups
    Blueberry, 19
    Honey, 31
    Simple, Basic, 17
    Simple, Cinnamon, 20
    Simple, Rich Demerara, 30

Tamales
    Delta Shrimp, 125
    Rich Pork and Cornmeal, *122*, 123
Tart, Roasted Fig Brown Butter, *244*, 245
Tartlet, Lemon Blackberry, with Sweet Mascarpone, 246, *247*
Tasso and White Bean Gratin, 204

Terrine, Fried Country, 126–27, *127*
Texas Campfire Dry Rub, 85
Tomato(es)
    and Bacon, Southern Bruschetta with, 47
    Cherry, and Basil, Broiled Flounder with, 175
    Lemon, and Basil, Scallop Crudo with, *154*, 155
    Smoked Ham and Rice Salad, 196, *197*
    Watermelon Gazpacho with Crabmeat, 147
Tuna
    Beach House Ceviche, *148*, 149
    Butter and Olive Oil–Poached, with Kumquats and Chiles, 176
Turkey Noodle Soup, 130–31, *131*
Turnips, Mustard-Marinated, 192

Uruguayan Spicy Baked Cheese, 40, *41*

Vanilla Wafers, 236
Vinaigrette, Lemon-Olive, 72
Vinegar, Easy Pickled Chile, 169

Walnut(s)
    McGaws' Extra-Bittersweet Chocolate Chunk Monster Cookies, *224*, 225
    Zucchini Bread, 232
Watermelon
    Beach House Ceviche, *148*, 149
    Gazpacho with Crabmeat, 147
Whipped Cream, Moonshine, Banana Pudding with, *234*, 235–36

White Chocolate
    and Bing Cherry Bread Pudding, 233
    Macadamia Blondies, 223
Wine. *See* Sparkling wine

Yogurt Sauce, Cucumbers, and Mint, Braised and Crispy Goat with, 108–9, *109*

Zucchini Walnut Bread, 232
Zucker Platschen (German Sugar Cookies), 216, *217*